CONTENTS

Bible Study at a Glance

Bible Story Script

➤ The Bible story script will help you prepare to tell the Bible story in your own words, or you may choose to show the Bible story video.

"Say" what?

➤ The "Leader" and "Say" segments are suggested lines designed to help a teacher easily segue from segment to segment. You can adapt, alter, or ignore any of the "Leader" and "Say" lines you want.

Small Group Opening

➤ A 15-minute time of opening activities is designed to introduce part of the day's session.

Large Group Leader

➤ A 30-minute time of teaching includes telling the Bible story, singing the theme song, reviewing the key passage and key passage song, discussing the timeline map, and more.

development show that children learn languages best during the childhood years and you have a recipe for success. Give children the opportunity to learn words in another language. While children will enjoy learning simple greetings, counting, and colors, also encourage them to learn some phrases with a purpose such as the chorus of "Jesus Loves Me."

Use Music from Other Cultures

Kids enjoy music and there are s many styles of music

The resources to help kids learn about other cultures are plentiful ...

as there are people groups on the planet. Give children the opportunity to listen to music from around the world. Even babies will benefit from this type of exposure.

The resources to help kids learn about other cultures are plentiful, but the greatest resource is a caring adult who will put effort into exploring those resources and then set a good example of understanding and loving all people. Will YOU be that one?

Excerpted from *in mINistry with kids*, Volume 5, Number 3.

Adapting to a Traditional Classroom

What do I do if I don't have a small group, large group format? It is easy to adapt *The Gospel Project for Kids*® to a traditional classroom.

Start each session by using the activities suggested in the Small Group Opening. Second, transition to the teaching in the Large Group Leader plan. Wrap up the day by reviewing the session through the activities in the Small Group Leader plan.

Tips for Adapting to the Traditional Classroom

1. You may want to rearrange some of the session. Example: Combine the key passage segments from Large Group Leader and Small Group Leader.
2. If you have space, lead the small group activities in one area of the room and the large group activities in another area of the room. This will help you and the kids transition.
3. Ask a helper to lead the session starter activity so you can prepare for the Large Group.
4. Only decorate the portion of your room where the Large Group Leader plan will be taught. Use a bulletin board or a few simple props.
5. Offer both activity options. Ask a co-leader to lead one activity while you lead the second choice to limit the number of kids in an activity.

A Sample Schedule in a Traditional Classroom

1. Welcome time
2. Activity page
3. Session starter
4. Countdown (clean up session starter supplies)
5. Introduce the session
6. Timeline map
7. Big picture question
8. Tell the Bible story
9. Sing
10. Discussion starter video
11. Bible story review and Bible skills
12. Key passage (read verse, sing song, key passage activity)
13. Activity option
14. Journal and prayer

Small Group Leader

➤ Use this 30-minute time to review the Bible story, build Bible skills, and encourage activity options, journaling, and more.

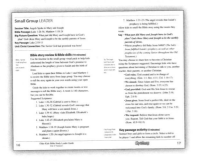

Suggested Times

➤ The times provided are suggested to allow you to complete the session plan in an hour and fifteen minutes. To lengthen the session, interact more with the kids or review previous sessions in more detail. To shorten the session, eliminate elements to fit your allotted time frame.

Themes

➤ In the Bible study hour, the themes have a small presence. The Large Group Leader is on the same journey as the kids in the theme location. The themes in Large Group can be played up or down to fit your teaching style and environment. You may choose to allow kids to assist in decorating by inviting early arrivers to draw or decorate additional decorations prior to class.

The Gospel: God's Plan for Me

➤ To allow you to choose when to share the gospel plan, Younger Kids and Older Kids includes a version of the gospel plan in each session.

Unit 7: EASTER

Big Picture Questions

Session 1: How did people act when they saw Jesus? People welcomed Jesus to Jerusalem as their King.

Session 2: What did Jesus do for sinners? Jesus' death and resurrection paid the penalty for sins and provided the promise of new life.

Session 3: What did Jesus do after He was raised from the dead? Jesus appeared to many people as proof that God had raised Jesus from the dead, and He is still alive today.

Unit 7: EASTER

Unit Description: God's plan for redemption, which began before creation, culminates with the death, burial, and resurrection of Jesus Christ. Jesus was welcomed as King but less than one week later was crucified by the people. Christ's sacrifice on the cross and His resurrection made it possible for people to have a pure relationship with God.

Unit Key Passage: Luke 24:46-47

Unit Christ Connection: God's plan for redemption is fulfilled through the death and resurrection of Jesus Christ.

Session 1: Jesus' Triumphal Entry
Matthew 21:1-17; Mark 11:1-11; Luke 19:28-44; John 12:12-19

Session 2: Jesus' Crucifixion and Resurrection
Matthew 26:36–28:10

Session 3: Jesus Appeared to Many People
Luke 24:36-49; John 20:19-29; Acts 1:3,9-11

Teacher BIBLE STUDY

It was time to celebrate the Passover. Many of God's people traveled to Jerusalem for the occasion. Jesus and His disciples traveled to Jerusalem as well. Jesus made a spectacular entrance into the city. He rode a donkey, and people laid branches and their robes on the ground in front of Him. The people welcoming Jesus into Jerusalem believed He was the promised Messiah, but they expected Him to be a political leader who would overthrow Roman oppression and set up an earthly throne. Jesus sent a different message when He entered Jerusalem.

First, Jesus entered Jerusalem. Read Zechariah 9:9. Jesus fulfilled this prophecy. He was the One Zechariah spoke about. Jesus was saying, "I am your King. But I am not here to fight. I come humbly. I am coming to save you." Jesus entered the temple and turned over the tables of the money changers and those selling doves. Read Isaiah 56:6-7. Jesus referred to Isaiah, declaring that His kingship would not just be over the Jews but over all people.

While Jesus was in the temple, He healed the blind and the lame. Check out the words of Isaiah 35:4-6. Jesus' actions declared, "I am not just your King; I am also your God."

Finally, the priests and the scribes in the temple heard the children worshiping Jesus as their King. "Do You hear what these children are saying?" they asked. Jesus replied, quoting Psalm 8:2: "Have you never read: You have prepared praise from the mouths of children and nursing infants?" Jesus gladly received their praise because He was worthy of their praise.

As we take a break from our chronological study to prepare for and celebrate Easter, help kids connect the dots between God's promises of a Messiah and Jesus' coming. Help them understand why Jesus came: to save the world from sin!

Older Kids BIBLE STUDY OVERVIEW

Session Title: Jesus' Triumphal Entry
Bible Passage: Matthew 21:1-17; Mark 11:1-11; Luke 19:28-44;
  John 12:12-19
Big Picture Question: How did people act when they saw Jesus? People
  welcomed Jesus to Jerusalem as their King.
Key Passage: Luke 24:46-47
Unit Christ Connection: God's plan for redemption is fulfilled through
  the death and resurrection of Jesus Christ.

Small Group Opening

Large Group Leader

Small Group Leader

Easter

The BIBLE STORY

Jesus' Triumphal Entry
Matthew 21:1-17; Mark 11:1-11; Luke 19:28-44; John 12:12-19

It was the time of year that the Israelites celebrated Passover. Many Israelites had traveled to Jerusalem to remember what God had done when He rescued His people from slavery in Egypt.

Jesus and His disciples traveled to Jerusalem, too. When they neared Bethphage (BETH fayj) and Bethany near the Mount of Olives, Jesus sent two of His disciples ahead into a village. "As soon as you enter the village," Jesus told them, "you will find a young donkey tied there. No one has ever sat on it. Untie it and bring it here. If anyone says to you 'Why are you doing this?' say, 'The Lord needs it.'" Jesus was going to fulfill a prophecy by the prophet Zechariah that said, "Look, your King is coming to you, gentle, and mounted on a donkey."

The disciples did as Jesus asked. As they untied the donkey, its owners said to them, "Why are you untying the donkey?" "The Lord needs it," they said. Then they brought the donkey to Jesus, threw their robes onto the donkey, and helped Jesus get on it. People were spreading their robes along the road, and others spread palm branches cut from the fields.

The whole crowd of the disciples began to praise God joyfully with a loud voice for all the miracles they had seen. "The King who comes in the name of the Lord is the blessed One. Peace in heaven and glory in the highest heaven! Hosanna!" The word *hosanna* means "save now." The people knew Jesus was their promised King!

Some of the Pharisees, the religious teachers, told Jesus, "Teacher, tell your disciples to be quiet!" Jesus answered, "If they did not praise Me, the rocks would praise Me!"

Jesus went to the temple complex in Jerusalem and drove out everyone buying and selling in the temple. He overturned the tables of the money changers and the chairs of those who were selling doves. He quoted the prophet Isaiah and said, "My house will be called a house of prayer for all nations. But you are making it into a den of thieves!"

While Jesus was in the temple complex, people who were blind and people who were lame came to Him. The blind and lame were not allowed to worship in the temple. Jesus healed them. The chief priests and scribes saw the miracles that Jesus performed and heard the children saying, "Hosanna to the Son of David!" or "Our king is here! Our king is here!" Even the kids knew Jesus was the promised King. The scribes and priests were angry and asked Jesus, "Do you hear what these children are saying? They are saying you are a king!"

"Yes," Jesus replied. "The Psalmist said: You have prepared praise from the mouths of children and nursing infants."

Jesus left them and went to the town of Bethany to spend the night.

Christ Connection: During Jesus' triumphal entry, the people welcomed Him as King. Jesus was the Messiah spoken about by the prophet Zechariah: "Look, your King is coming to you; He is righteous and victorious, humble and riding on a donkey, on a colt, the foal of a donkey" (Zechariah 9:9).

Small Group OPENING

Session Title: Jesus' Triumphal Entry
Bible Passage: Matthew 21:1-17; Mark 11:1-11; Luke 19:28-44;
John 12:12-19
Big Picture Question: How did people act when they saw Jesus? People welcomed Jesus to Jerusalem as their King.
Key Passage: Luke 24:46-47
Unit Christ Connection: God's plan for redemption is fulfilled through the death and resurrection of Jesus Christ.

Welcome time

Use this time to collect the offering, fill out attendance sheets, and help new kids connect to your group. Ask each kid to share one word that describes Jesus. Ask each kid why he chose the word he chose.

- "Palms of Praise" activity page, 1 per kid
- pencils

Activity page (5 minutes)

Say • In today's Bible story, you will hear how the people described Jesus. People in the Bible had a variety of responses to Jesus. Some were happy to see Him. Some were grateful for Him. Some were angry at Him.

Help kids complete the activity page "Palms of Praise." (*Answers: died for me, gave me a home, Christian friends, the Bible.*) Encourage kids to share their responses.

- chart paper
- markers
- rock

Session starter (10 minutes)

Option 1: Kingly ABCs

Form two groups and provide each group with chart paper and markers. Explain that you will drop a rock onto an alphabet chart. The letter the rock lands on or closest to will be the letter for that round of play. Challenge each group to

Older Kids Bible Study Leader Guide
Unit 7 • Session 1
© 2012 LifeWay Christian Resources

Tip: Print the alphabet on the chart paper prior to class. You may want to print the letters in a random order.

create a list of words beginning with the chosen letter that describe a king. Toss the rock and change the letter every 45–60 seconds. The team with the most kingly words wins.

Say • Some of the words on your lists describe the type of king the Israelites were looking for. Some of the Israelite people thought that Jesus might be that type of king. Listen closely to today's Bible story to discover what type of king Jesus truly is.

• palm branches of your choice (real, plastic, or paper)
• music of your choice

Options: Substitute coats or pieces of fabric for palm branches.

Lead kids to sing a song together. When you stop singing, that is the cue for the kids to stop singing and pick up a branch.

Allow the eliminated player to rotate back in the game on the next round.

Tip: If kids become too rough, lead them to play the game sitting down in a circle with all the branches piled in the middle.

Option 2: Palm branch grab

Place a pile of palm branches on the floor or on a table. You need one less palm branch than the number of kids playing. As the music plays, kids will walk around the pile. When the music stops the kids will scramble to grab a palm branch and shout "hosanna."

Allow the eliminated player to start and stop the music on the next round. Continue playing the game until only one or two kids remain.

Say • *Hosanna* means "save now." The people shouted hosanna in today's Bible story. The Israelites wanted someone to save them from the people who ruled over them, the Romans.

Transition to large group

Large Group LEADER

Session Title: Jesus' Triumphal Entry
Bible Passage: Matthew 21:1-17; Mark 11:1-11; Luke 19:28-44; John 12:12-19
Big Picture Question: How did people act when they saw Jesus? People welcomed Jesus to Jerusalem as their King.
Key Passage: Luke 24:46-47
Unit Christ Connection: God's plan for redemption is fulfilled through the death and resurrection of Jesus Christ.

• room decorations

Suggested Theme Decorating Ideas: Decorate your room using elements from the Easter story. Place an empty cross in one area of the stage and an empty tomb or large rock in another area. A cross and tomb can be drawn on long paper and attached to the walls. If you are in the middle of another unit's theme, add the Easter elements to the existing theme.

Countdown

• countdown video

Show the countdown video as your kids arrive, and set it to end as large group time begins.

• coats, palm branches, and rocks or pebbles

Option: Use strips of fabric if you do not have biblical coats or clothing.

Tip: Each week the Large Group Leader knows what is going on but refuses to tell the kids. You may choose to play up this element to entertain the kids.

Introduce the session (1 minute)

[Scatter coats and palm branches across the teaching area. Large Group Leader enters, stepping on the coats and branches. Also have a pile of rocks or pebbles on the stage.]

Leader • What are all of these coats and palm branches doing on the floor? Why would someone throw his coat on the ground instead of hanging it up? Do your parents let you throw your clothes on the ground? This is not normal. And a pile of rocks. Why would you bring rocks inside and pile them up here? I wonder what is going on.

Do you know? No, you don't. What about you? Oh, some of you think you do know what all of this means. Well, guess what? I do know what it means. But I'm not going to tell you yet, and you may not guess yet. I will say that it is connected to our Bible story. Come look at our timeline map and see if you can find a clue about these palm branches, coats, and rocks.

• Timeline Map

Timeline map (1 minute)

Explain to kids that you are pausing in the chronological journey through God's plan to celebrate Easter. Point out Creation, the last session you taught, Jesus' birth, and today's Bible story picture on the timeline map.

Leader •I see in our Bible story picture a lot of people waving palm branches. And the people have put their coats on the road for a donkey carrying a man to walk across. Interesting! Do you know what it all means yet? Here is another clue! The timeline says today's Bible story is about Jesus and His triumphal entry. According to our timeline, our Bible story begins in Matthew 21.

Big picture question (1 minute)

Leader •I have the perfect big picture question for our Bible story. Are you ready for today's big picture question? If you are ready, I want to hear you say "Praise the Lord" when I count to three. One. Two. Three.

Pause and allow the kids to respond. You may wish to repeat if the kids aren't enthusiastic.

Leader •You are ready! Here is the big picture question: *How did people act when they saw Jesus?* OK, we need to open our Bibles to Matthew 21 and locate the answer to our big picture question.

Tell the Bible story (10 minutes)

- "Jesus' Triumphal Entry" video
- Bibles, 1 per kid
- Bible Story Picture Slide or Poster (enhanced CD)
- Big Picture Question Slide or Poster (enhanced CD)

Open your Bible to Matthew 21 and tell the Bible story in your own words, or show the Bible story video "Jesus' Triumphal Entry."

Even if you are showing the video, help every kid locate the Scripture in the Bible. This will help build Bible skills as well as help kids connect that the Bible story is from the Bible.

Leader • Who remembers our big picture question? Our big picture question is, *How did people act when they saw Jesus?* The big picture answer is, *People welcomed Jesus to Jerusalem as their King.* The Israelites really wanted a king to save them from being ruled by leaders from another kingdom. Hundreds of years before Jesus' birth, most of the Israelites quit following God. As a consequence of their sin, other kingdoms captured them. When Jesus came to earth, the Israelites were still being ruled by another kingdom—the Roman Empire. The Israelites believed that the Messiah would come as a king to save them from earthly rulers. They were excited to see Jesus enter Jerusalem. They wanted a king. They wanted the Messiah the prophets had told about to come and help them be free again.

But the people didn't understand that Jesus came to earth to save them from something much worse than a human ruler. Jesus came to earth to save people from sin. God's plan was to send Jesus to earth to pay the penalty for sin—to die on the cross so we could be forgiven.

Unlike the people who were praising and welcoming Jesus, the religious leaders did not like Jesus. The people liked Jesus, and that made the religious leaders worry. They didn't want the people to praise Jesus by waving palm branches and shouting "Hosanna!"

What did Jesus tell the leaders when they told Jesus to make the people stop praising Him? Jesus said that if the people didn't praise Him the rocks would praise Him. Jesus is the Messiah, the King of all kings. If people don't bring Him praise, creation will bring Him praise.

The religious leaders became upset with Jesus when Jesus kicked all the money changers out of the temple. The money changers had turned part of the temple complex into a place of business. The temple was supposed to be a place of worship and prayer.

Jesus also healed the blind and the lame people in the temple complex. Jesus demonstrated that He was the Son of God and had the power and authority to heal people. The religious leaders were upset that the kids were praising Jesus. They did not like that all the people were following Jesus. They began to look for a way to get rid of Jesus. We will hear more about that next week. Tell me again, *How did people act when they saw Jesus? People welcomed Jesus to Jerusalem as their King.*

The Gospel: God's Plan for Me (optional)

Using Scripture and the guide provided, share with kids the plan of salvation. Provide kids with an opportunity to respond and counselors to speak with one-on-one.

• Key Passage Slide or Poster (enhanced CD)
• "Luke 24:46-47" song

Key passage (5 minutes)

Leader •Jesus came to earth to rescue us from our sins. He came to die on the cross for the sins of people everywhere. Let's read our key passage for this unit.
Lead kids to read the key passage together. You may choose to form two groups and lead each group to read every other line of the key passage. Sing "Luke 24:46-47."

Discussion starter video (5 minutes)

• "Unit 7 Session 1" discussion starter video

Leader • *How did people act when they saw Jesus? People welcomed Jesus to Jerusalem as their King.* The way we welcome Jesus is different than the people in our story today. How do people respond to Jesus in today's world? What are some ways we can welcome Jesus today?

Allow kids to provide a few answers. Show the "Unit 7 Session 1" discussion starter video.

Leader • What would you do? In our Bible story we heard that the people welcomed Jesus but the religious leaders didn't. What would you do if you were one of the other kids at the party? Would you welcome a new person?

Sing (5 minutes)

• "Jesus Saves" song

Leader • Next week we will hear more about how Jesus is our Savior and rescues us. Sadly, not everyone understands or believes that Jesus is Savior and King. But we know that He is, and we can worship Jesus as our Savior and King. Join me in singing our unit theme song.

Sing "Jesus Saves."

Prayer (2 minutes)

Leader • So someone tell me, what do all the palm branches, coats, and rocks remind us of? Excellent listening today! You are right! *How did people act when they saw Jesus? People welcomed Jesus to Jerusalem as their King.* Easter is a special time for us to remember the sacrifice Jesus made for us. We'll talk more about that this Easter season. After I pray, watch your small group leader for the signal to go to your small group area.

Close in prayer.

Dismiss to small groups

The Gospel: God's Plan for Me

Ask kids if they have ever heard the word *gospel*. Clarify that the word *gospel* means "good news." It is the message about Christ, the kingdom of God, and salvation. Use the following guide to share the gospel with kids.

God rules. Explain to kids that the Bible tells us God created everything, and He is in charge of everything. Invite a volunteer to read Genesis 1:1 from the Bible. Read Revelation 4:11 or Colossians 1:16-17 aloud and explain what these verses mean.

We sinned. Tell kids that since the time of Adam and Eve, everyone has chosen to disobey God. (Romans 3:23) The Bible calls this sin. Because God is holy, God cannot be around sin. Sin separates us from God and deserves God's punishment of death. (Romans 6:23)

God provided. Choose a child to read John 3:16 aloud. Say that God sent His Son, Jesus, the perfect solution to our sin problem, to rescue us from the punishment we deserve. It's something we, as sinners, could never earn on our own. Jesus alone saves us. Read and explain Ephesians 2:8-9.

Jesus gives. Share with kids that Jesus lived a perfect life, died on the cross for our sins, and rose again. Because Jesus gave up His life for us, we can be welcomed into God's family for eternity. This is the best gift ever! Read Romans 5:8; 2 Corinthians 5:21; or 1 Peter 3:18.

We respond. Tell kids that they can respond to Jesus. Read Romans 10:9-10,13. Review these aspects of our response: Believe in your heart that Jesus alone saves you through what He's already done on the cross. Repent, turning from self and sin to Jesus. Tell God and others that your faith is in Jesus.

Offer to talk with any child who is interested in responding to Jesus.

Small Group LEADER

Session Title: Jesus' Triumphal Entry
Bible Passage: Matthew 21:1-17; Mark 11:1-11; Luke 19:28-44;
John 12:12-19
Big Picture Question: How did people act when they saw Jesus? People
welcomed Jesus to Jerusalem as their King.
Key Passage: Luke 24:46-47
Unit Christ Connection: God's plan for redemption is fulfilled through
the death and resurrection of Jesus Christ.

· Bibles, 1 per kid
· Small Group Visual
  Pack
· paper
· markers or crayons

Bible story review & Bible skills (10 minutes)

Help kids create a storyboard to review today's Bible story.
Each piece should depict one part of the story. Line up the
pictures in order and allow kids to share what is happening
in each piece. Kids may work individually, in pairs, or in
trios to create each scene.

Possible storyboard scenes:
- Jesus talking with disciples at the Mount of Olives
  (Matt. 21:1-2)
- Disciples getting the colt (Matt. 21:2-3,6-7)
- People spreading coats on the ground (Matt. 21:8)
- People praising Jesus as He enters Jerusalem
  (Matt. 21:9)
- Jesus healing the blind and lame (Matt. 21:14)
- Children praising Jesus in the temple complex
  (Matt. 21:15)
- Jesus talking to the religious leaders (Matt. 21:15-16)

Allow kids to take turns narrating the scenes they depicted.

Say • *How did people act when they saw Jesus? People
welcomed Jesus to Jerusalem as their King.*
- Which prophet spoke about Jesus' entrance into
  Jerusalem? (*Jesus was the Messiah spoken about by*

the prophet Zechariah: "Look, your King is coming to you; He is righteous and victorious, humble and riding on a donkey, on a colt, the foal of a donkey" [Zechariah 9:9].)

Lead kids to find Zechariah 9:9 in their Bibles and read the verse aloud.

Say • During His time on earth, Jesus fulfilled many prophecies made by the Old Testament prophets.

You may opt to review the gospel plan with boys and girls.

Tip: Provide kids with an opportunity to respond if they need to talk with someone or ask questions about becoming a Christian.

- **God rules.** God created and is in charge of everything. (Gen. 1:1; Rev. 4:11; Col. 1:16-17)
- **We sinned.** Since Adam and Eve, everyone has chosen to disobey God. (Rom. 3:23; 6:23)
- **God provided.** God sent His Son Jesus to rescue us from the punishment we deserve. (John 3:16; Eph. 2:8-9)
- **Jesus gives.** Jesus lived a perfect life, died on the cross for our sins, and rose again so we can be welcomed into God's family. (Rom. 5:8; 2 Cor. 5:21; 1 Pet. 3:18)
- **We respond.** Believe that Jesus alone saves you. Repent. Tell God that your faith is in Jesus. (Rom. 10:9-10,13)

• Key Passage Poster (enhanced CD)

Tip: Keep the rhythm simple to assist kids in memorizing the passage. A complicated pattern can distract or frustrate the kids.

Key passage activity (5 minutes)

Read the key passage with a rhythm that fits the flow of the passage. Add claps, pauses, leg slaps, snaps, and foot taps to create the cadence. You may choose to form pairs and give each pair a phrase to create a rhythm for.

Say • Our key passage is a reminder that Jesus, the Messiah, sacrificed His life for people of all nations. If you have questions about Jesus' life, death, and resurrection, please ask one of the adults here today.

Activity choice (10 minutes)

Option 1: Celebration streamers

Invite kids to cut 10 or 12 pieces of crepe paper. Stack the pieces together and wrap tape around the end of the stack. Explain to kids that you will read a scenario. If the scenario calls for celebration, kids should stand, wave their streamers, and cheer as if the event is actually happening.

- crepe paper streamers
- tape
- scissors

- hitting a home run
- breaking a windshield with a baseball
- being benched from the ballgame for a bad attitude
- attending a birthday party
- making an A on a test
- cleaning your room
- breaking your favorite video game
- witnessing a friend become a Christian
- having a new sibling
- getting your feelings hurt by a friend
- being elected class president

Say • *How did people act when they saw Jesus? People welcomed Jesus to Jerusalem as their King.* Jesus' entrance into Jerusalem was a time of celebration. We can celebrate and remember all that Jesus has done. What is something Jesus has done for you that you can celebrate?

- long sheets of paper or poster board, 4 pieces
- markers
- Bibles
- music of your choice

As each kid shares, encourage kids to celebrate what Jesus has done by waving their streamers and cheering.

Tip: If your third and fourth graders need more structure, assign kids a station to start at and announce when to rotate to another station.

Option 2: Prayer stations

Create four stations around your teaching area. Each station needs one long sheet of paper, markers, and room for kids to kneel to write. Write a prayer station prompt on each piece of paper. Leave space for kids to add their responses.

Options: If you want
to add a station
for confession
or repentance of
sins, provide kids
with individual
papers and pencils.
Encourage kids to
write their prayer of
repentance on the
piece of paper, wad
it up, and toss it into
the trash can.

Assign a helper
to each station
to assist kids as
needed.

Sample Station Prompts:
- I praise God for …
- I thank God for …
- God is …
- God, please …

Say • *How did people act when they saw Jesus? People welcomed Jesus to Jerusalem as their King.* Jesus explained to the people in the temple that God's house, the temple, was meant to be a place people could worship and pray to God. People had turned part of the temple complex into a place of business. You can worship and pray to God anywhere, anytime. And today we are going to spend some time praying and worshiping God.

Inform kids that you created "prayer stations" around the area for kids to visit. Each station focuses on a different type of prayer. As the music plays softly in the background, kids may move between the stations, writing their thoughts on the paper at each station. Close the activity by allowing a couple of volunteers to pray aloud.

Journal and prayer (5 minutes)

- pencils
- journals
- Bibles
- Journal Page,
  1 per kid (enhanced CD)
- "The Prophecy of the Coming King" activity page,
  1 per kid

Ask kids to think about a time they did not welcome Jesus into a part of their lives. Encourage kids to write about that time and how they hope to respond differently in the future.

Invite kids to journal how they want to welcome Jesus this week.

Say • *How did people act when they saw Jesus? People welcomed Jesus to Jerusalem as their King.*

Close the journal time by praying for boys and girls to welcome Jesus into all areas of their life.

If time allows, help kids complete the activity page, "The Prophecy of the Coming King."

Teacher BIBLE STUDY

Why did Jesus have to die? Why couldn't God just say, "You are forgiven"? God is just and requires due payment for sin. To simply forgive sin without requiring a payment would be unjust. According to God's Word, the payment of sin is death. (Rom. 6:23) But not only is God just, He is also loving. That is why Jesus was willing to die in our place. He loved us.

God's law for the people was plain. Read Deuteronomy 6:5. But God's people, and all people, have broken the law. We have loved other things more than we love God. That is sin.

Jesus' purpose for coming to earth was to save us from our sin. (Matt. 1:21) Jesus came to die to show God's love to us (Rom. 5:7-8) so that whoever believes in Him might not perish but have eternal life. (John 3:16) Jesus came to die so that we would be forgiven. (Eph. 1:7) Jesus came to die to bring us to God. (1 Pet. 3:18)

Jesus died on the cross to satisfy the wrath of God toward sin. Jesus' resurrection proved that God was satisfied with Jesus' sacrifice. If Jesus had died but not been raised up, He would have been like other military leaders who died without a throne. (Acts 5:33-37) But Jesus conquered death, just as He said He would. (John 2:19-21)

Jesus' resurrection gives us hope for our resurrection. (Rom. 6:5) And Romans 8:11 says that the same Spirit that raised Jesus from the dead will raise our bodies to life.

Jesus' crucifixion and resurrection are not the end of the story, but the climax. Everything that was written about Jesus in the Old Testament and spoken by the prophets was coming true. As you teach kids this Bible story, emphasize the gospel: the good news of who Jesus is and what He has done.

Older Kids BIBLE STUDY OVERVIEW

Session Title: Jesus' Crucifixion and Resurrection
Bible Passage: Matthew 26:36–28:10
Big Picture Question: What did Jesus do for sinners? Jesus' death and resurrection paid the penalty for sins and provided the promise of new life.
Key Passage: Luke 24:46-47
Unit Christ Connection: God's plan for redemption is fulfilled through the death and resurrection of Jesus Christ.

Small Group Opening

Large Group Leader

Small Group Leader

The BIBLE STORY

Jesus' Crucifixion and Resurrection
Matthew 26:36–28:10

Jesus came with His disciples to a place called Gethsemane (geth SEM uh nih). He said to them, "Sit here while I go over there and pray." Jesus took Peter, James, and John with Him, and He became very sad and troubled. He said to them, "I am overcome with sadness; I feel as if I am dying. Wait here and stay awake with Me."

Jesus went a little farther. He fell facedown and prayed to God, "Father! If it is possible, take this suffering away from Me. But only if it is part of Your plan." Jesus came back and found the disciples asleep. He asked Peter, "Couldn't you stay awake with Me for one hour?"

Again, Jesus went away and prayed to God. Then He found His disciples sleeping. He said to them, "Are you still asleep? Get up, for it is almost time. Someone is going to betray Me."

Suddenly Judas arrived. A large crowd carrying swords and clubs was with him. Judas kissed Jesus so the crowd would know who Jesus was. The men grabbed Jesus and arrested Him. Jesus asked, "Am I a criminal? All of these things that are happening are fulfilling what the prophets wrote." Then all of Jesus' followers ran away.

The men who arrested Jesus led Him to the house of Caiaphas, the high priest. The priests and high council were trying to find a reason to kill Jesus, but they could not. The high priest asked, "Are you the Messiah, the Son of God?"

Jesus replied, "Yes, that's right." The high priest said, "Ah ha! He has spoken against God." Caiaphas and the council did not want to believe Jesus was God's Son. They said Jesus was lying, but Jesus cannot lie! The crowd answered, "He deserves to die!" They spit in Jesus' face and beat Him.

The next morning, the chief priests and elders led Jesus to Pilate, the governor. "Are you the King of the Jews?" Pilate asked.

"Yes, that's right," Jesus replied. The men accused Jesus of various crimes, but Jesus said nothing.

"What should I do with Jesus the Messiah?" Pilate asked the crowd.

They all answered, "Crucify Him!" Pilate did not think Jesus had done anything wrong, but he handed Jesus over to them and said, "Do whatever you want."

The governor's soldiers took off Jesus' clothes and put a scarlet robe on Him. They made a crown out of thorns and put it on His head. Then they mocked Him, "Here is the King of the Jews!" Then they beat Him and led Him away to be killed.

The soldiers nailed Jesus to a cross. They put a sign above His head that said: THIS IS JESUS, THE KING OF THE JEWS. Two criminals were crucified next to Him.

From noon until three in the afternoon, darkness covered the land. Then Jesus cried out, "My God, My God, why have You forsaken Me?" Jesus shouted again with a loud voice and then He died. Suddenly, the curtain in the temple sanctuary split in two, from top to bottom, and there was an earthquake. One of the men guarding Jesus' body said, "This man really was God's Son!"

That evening, Jesus was buried in a rich man's tomb cut into a rock. A stone was sealed in front of the tomb so that no one could steal Jesus' body.

Three days later, on the first day of the week, Mary Magdalene (MAG duh leen) and the other Mary went to see the tomb. Suddenly there was an earthquake as an angel of the Lord came to the tomb. He rolled back the stone and was sitting on it. The guards were so afraid that they fainted.

The angel spoke to the women, "Don't be afraid! I know you are looking for Jesus, but He is not here. He has been resurrected, just like He said He would. In fact, He is going ahead of you into Galilee."

The women left the tomb quickly and with great joy. They ran to tell the disciples the news. Just then Jesus met them. "Good morning!" He said. The women worshiped Him. "Don't be afraid," Jesus told them. "Go tell My disciples to meet Me in Galilee. They will see Me there."

Christ Connection: The crucifixion and resurrection of Jesus is the center of the gospel. We deserve to die because of our sin, but Jesus died in our place. He was the blood sacrifice made once and for all for the forgiveness of sin. God was pleased with Jesus' sacrifice and raised Jesus from the dead to reign as King over all creation. We are forgiven only through Jesus. (Acts 4:12)

Easter

Small Group OPENING

Session Title: Jesus' Crucifixion and Resurrection
Bible Passage: Matthew 26:36–28:10
Big Picture Question: What did Jesus do for sinners? Jesus' death and resurrection paid the penalty for sins and provided the promise of new life.
Key Passage: Luke 24:46-47
Unit Christ Connection: God's plan for redemption is fulfilled through the death and resurrection of Jesus Christ.

- Bible (optional)

Welcome time

Collect the offering, fill out attendance sheets, and help new kids connect to your group during this time. Ask kids to tell you in their own words the definition of the word *sinner*. You may choose to read Romans 3:23 and 6:23 to review what the Bible says about sin.

- "Resurrection Code" activity page, 1 per kid
- pencils

Activity page (5 minutes)

Guide boys and girls to complete the "Resurrection Code" activity page. (*Answer: promise of new life*)

Say • Today we are celebrating Easter. Easter is the time Christians celebrate Jesus' resurrection. Easter is also the time we remember the sacrifice Jesus made by dying for our sins. We have the promise of new life because of Jesus' death, burial, and resurrection. What is one way you or your family celebrate(s) the resurrection of Jesus?

- paper
- pen
- Write tasks on slips of paper.

Session starter (10 minutes)

Option 1: Can't say no

Allow kids to take turns drawing a task to perform. No one should say no to performing their task. To prevent kids from feeling embarrassed, allow kids to volunteer to participate. Remember the goal is for kids to perform a task, so keep all tasks attainable.

Sample activities:

- Tie a friend's shoe.
- Find a friend and sing the ABCs.
- High-five two people.
- Turn around and sit down.
- Sing "Jesus Loves Me."
- Do three jumping jacks.
- Count backward from 10 to 1.

Say • Do you think Jesus ever said no to doing what God wanted Him to do? (*No!*)

- Jesus never said no to following God's plan. Even as He gave His life for our sin, Jesus always desired to do God's will.
- Jesus always said no to sin but yes to God.

• small rocks or similar item

Option 2: Easter create it

Select a volunteer to use the objects provided to create an item related to today's Bible story. Challenge the remaining kids to guess what the item is. Give the volunteer a 30-second head start before anyone can guess.

Challenge kids to create the following items: a cross, a sword, the temple curtain, and the angel of the Lord.

Say • Each of the items you created is found in today's Bible story. Today we will see God's plan to rescue people from sin forever. Does anyone know why we are using rocks to create our items? A very large rock is also in today's Bible story.

Transition to large group

Large Group LEADER

Session Title: Jesus' Crucifixion and Resurrection
Bible Passage: Matthew 26:36–28:10
Big Picture Question: What did Jesus do for sinners? Jesus' death and resurrection paid the penalty for sins and provided the promise of new life.
Key Passage: Luke 24:46-47
Unit Christ Connection: God's plan for redemption is fulfilled through the death and resurrection of Jesus Christ.

Countdown

• countdown video

Show the countdown video as your kids arrive, and set it to end as large group time begins.

Introduce the session (1 minute)

[Prior to large group, completely clear the stage. The teaching area should be as empty as possible without compromising your ability to teach. Remove the kids' seats to create a large empty space. Try to extend the "empty" effect to the entire room by removing anything you can.]

Leader • What happened to our room? Where are your seats? Where is …? And that is missing too? Everything is missing! Do you all know what happened? You don't? Can you guess who does know what happened? I do!

OK, everyone have a seat on the floor, and I will help you solve this mystery. Have you ever seen our room so empty before? Do you think this has anything to do with our Bible story today? Yes. You do. Then you need to consult the timeline map to see what our Bible story is.

Timeline map (1 minute)

• Timeline Map

Leader • Last week we heard the Bible story of Jesus

entering Jerusalem. ***How did people act when they saw Jesus? People welcomed Jesus to Jerusalem as their King.*** The people were very excited about Jesus' entrance into Jerusalem. How did the religious leaders respond to Jesus? Right! They were upset and did not like how the people praised Jesus. Our story today starts a few days after Jesus entered Jerusalem.

Big picture question (1 minute)

Leader • Our big picture today is, ***What did Jesus do for sinners?*** We have been talking for a long time about God's plan to send Jesus to rescue people from sin. Today we are going to see how Jesus paid the price for our sin. We will discover, ***What did Jesus do for sinners?***

Tell the Bible story (10 minutes)

- "Jesus' Crucifixion and Resurrection" video
- Bibles
- Bible Story Picture Slide or Poster (enhanced CD)
- Big Picture Question Slide or Poster (enhanced CD)

Open your Bible to Matthew 26 and tell the Bible story in your own words, or show the Bible story video "Jesus' Crucifixion and Resurrection."

Leader • The religious leaders decided that they wanted to get rid of Jesus. They were tired of the people praising Jesus and following Him. So they created a plan and paid one of Jesus' disciples to betray Him.

The religious leaders refused to accept who Jesus truly was. When Jesus told them He was the Son of God, they didn't believe Him. They proclaimed Him guilty of blasphemy. *Blasphemy* is an attitude of disrespect for God. They believed that Jesus had committed a crime by claiming to be fully God, but Jesus hadn't.

Is Jesus the Son of God? YES! Is Jesus fully God? YES! But the religious leaders didn't believe it. They convinced the crowd that Jesus should die. Sadly, in less than a week people went from praising Jesus to hating Him.

Jesus knew it was time to provide the way for people to be forgiven of their sins. Why did Jesus have to die? The Bible tells us that sin requires a payment, a blood sacrifice. To fully pay for our sin, Jesus had to be our blood sacrifice. Jesus could pay the price for us because He did not sin.

To be crucified was the worst way to die during that time. But Jesus was willing to pay that price to follow God's plan. Jesus was willing to die for us—to redeem us.

The people thought crucifying Jesus was their idea for getting rid of Him, but Jesus' death had been God's plan all along. His death would save sinners.

What did Jesus do for sinners? Jesus' death and resurrection paid the penalty for sins and provided the promise of new life. For Christians, the death and resurrection of Jesus is a time of remembrance and celebration. We remember the sacrifice Jesus made to pay for our sin. We remember the pain He suffered for us. But we celebrate that Jesus defeated sin and death. We celebrate that we can be forgiven of our sin. We celebrate that Jesus is alive and we will see Him one day. We celebrate that we have the promise of new life. We celebrate that we can be free from sin and spend eternity with Jesus.

We are so blessed to know the entire story, but the followers of Jesus weren't sure what was happening. The followers of Jesus did not understand what Jesus told them about His resurrection. Imagine the surprise and the joy the women felt when they heard that Jesus was alive. It was wonderful news to hear the angel announce that Jesus was alive. God had raised Jesus from the dead. What an even bigger surprise for the women to actually see Jesus! What do you think the women felt? The women probably felt all of those emotions. What do you feel when you think about Jesus' resurrection? I am grateful that Jesus came and died in my place.

Sing (5 minutes)

• "Jesus Saves" song

Leader • Let's celebrate the resurrection of Jesus by singing our theme song. Jesus is alive! Because He died and rose again, we can sing and tell the world that Jesus is our Savior! Only Jesus can save us from our sin.

Lead kids to sing "Jesus Saves."

Key passage (5 minutes)

• Key Passage Slide or Poster (enhanced CD)
• "Luke 24:46-47" song

Leader • Our key passage this unit tells the story of Jesus' death and resurrection. When I give the signal, everyone on the left half of the room should read the key passage. I'll give the signal again and everyone on the right side will read the key passage.

Lead the boys and girls to read the key passage. Sing "Luke 24:46-47."

The Gospel: God's Plan for Me (optional)

• Bible

Leader • *What did Jesus do for sinners? Jesus' death and resurrection paid the penalty for sins and provided the promise of new life.* God is just and must punish sin. That is why we are grateful that God graciously sent His Son to pay for our sin. God loves us and provided the way for us to be forgiven of our sin.

Using Scripture and the plan provided, review how to become a Christian. Give kids the opportunity to respond.

Be sensitive to kids who may be emotional following today's Bible story. Urge counselors to allow the kid to direct the conversation. This will help them determine what each kid needs.

Discussion starter video (5 minutes)

• "Unit 7 Session 2" discussion starter video

Leader • Why do people celebrate Easter? Someone tell me why you celebrate Easter. Good answers. Check out this video and we'll talk about it afterward.

Show the "Unit 7 Session 2" discussion starter video.

Leader • Interesting answers. What do you think?

Allow a few kids to respond.

Leader • Why do Christians celebrate Easter? Do Christians and non-Christians celebrate Easter in different ways? Do they celebrate for different reasons?

Who remembers our big picture question? *What did Jesus do for sinners? Jesus' death and resurrection paid the penalty for sins and provided the promise of new life.* Does your answer to the question about why you celebrate Easter change when you think about the big picture question?

Allow a few kids to respond and close the discussion when kids have arrived at a good conclusion.

Prayer (2 minutes)

Leader • Have you figured it out yet? Do you know why our room is so empty today? Yes! Our room is empty to remind us that the tomb—Jesus' tomb—is empty. Jesus is alive! Shout that phrase with me. *Jesus is alive!*

We are blessed that God demonstrated His grace and His love for us when He sent His Son to die for our sins. *What did Jesus do for sinners? Jesus' death and resurrection paid the penalty for sins and provided the promise of new life.* After I pray, watch your small group leader for your signal to go to small group.

Close in prayer. Thank and praise God for sending Jesus.

Dismiss to small groups

The Gospel: God's Plan for Me

Ask kids if they have ever heard the word *gospel*. Clarify that the word *gospel* means "good news." It is the message about Christ, the kingdom of God, and salvation. Use the following guide to share the gospel with kids.

God rules. Explain to kids that the Bible tells us God created everything, and He is in charge of everything. Invite a volunteer to read Genesis 1:1 from the Bible. Read Revelation 4:11 or Colossians 1:16-17 aloud and explain what these verses mean.

We sinned. Tell kids that since the time of Adam and Eve, everyone has chosen to disobey God. (Romans 3:23) The Bible calls this sin. Because God is holy, God cannot be around sin. Sin separates us from God and deserves God's punishment of death. (Romans 6:23)

God provided. Choose a child to read John 3:16 aloud. Say that God sent His Son, Jesus, the perfect solution to our sin problem, to rescue us from the punishment we deserve. It's something we, as sinners, could never earn on our own. Jesus alone saves us. Read and explain Ephesians 2:8-9.

Jesus gives. Share with kids that Jesus lived a perfect life, died on the cross for our sins, and rose again. Because Jesus gave up His life for us, we can be welcomed into God's family for eternity. This is the best gift ever! Read Romans 5:8; 2 Corinthians 5:21; or 1 Peter 3:18.

We respond. Tell kids that they can respond to Jesus. Read Romans 10:9-10,13. Review these aspects of our response: Believe in your heart that Jesus alone saves you through what He's already done on the cross. Repent, turning from self and sin to Jesus. Tell God and others that your faith is in Jesus.

Offer to talk with any child who is interested in responding to Jesus.

Small Group LEADER

Session Title: Jesus' Crucifixion and Resurrection
Bible Passage: Matthew 26:36–28:10
Big Picture Question: What did Jesus do for sinners? Jesus' death and resurrection paid the penalty for sins and provided the promise of new life.
Key Passage: Luke 24:46-47
Unit Christ Connection: God's plan for redemption is fulfilled through the death and resurrection of Jesus Christ.

- Bibles, 1 per kid
- Small Group Visual Pack
- tape
- small pieces of paper or index cards
- marker

Bible story review & Bible skills (10 minutes)

Write the names of various Bible people from today's Bible story on separate pieces of paper. Tape a Bible person's name on each kid's back. If you have more kids than names, assign some kids the same name. Instruct kids to ask only yes-no questions to discover what names are on their backs.

After boys and girls have discovered all the Bible people, invite boys and girls to ask any questions they have about the Bible story. Review the Bible story.

Say • *What did Jesus do for sinners? Jesus' death and resurrection paid the penalty for sins and provided the promise of new life.*

• Who made the blood sacrifice once and for all? (*Jesus made the blood sacrifice once and for all for the forgiveness of sin. God was pleased with Jesus' sacrifice and raised Jesus from the dead to reign as King over all creation. We are forgiven only through Jesus.*)

Lead boys and girls to read Acts 4:12. Explain that Jesus is the only way of salvation.

As time allows, you may choose to review the gospel plan with boys and girls. Be sensitive to the emotions kids may be feeling after today's Bible story. Provide kids with an opportunity to respond without pressure.

- **God rules.** God created and is in charge of everything. (Gen. 1:1; Rev. 4:11; Col. 1:16-17)
- **We sinned.** Since Adam and Eve, everyone has chosen to disobey God. (Rom. 3:23; 6:23)
- **God provided.** God sent His Son Jesus to rescue us from the punishment we deserve. (John 3:16; Eph. 2:8-9)
- **Jesus gives.** Jesus lived a perfect life, died on the cross for our sins, and rose again so we can be welcomed into God's family. (Rom. 5:8; 2 Cor. 5:21; 1 Pet. 3:18)
- **We respond.** Believe that Jesus alone saves you. Repent. Tell God that your faith is in Jesus. (Rom. 10:9-10,13)

· Key Passage Poster (enhanced CD)
· chart paper
· marker

Note: Challenge adult and teen helpers to memorize the key passage too.

Key passage activity (5 minutes)

Allow kids to create a code for the key passage. Guide kids to replace key words or phrases from the passage with a symbol from today's story (cross, tomb, disciple, temple, and so forth). Record their code on chart paper.

Say • Next week is our last week to work on our key passage. Practice the passage at home this week and next week we'll see how many of us can quote it.

· small foam ball
· scissors
· masking or painter's tape

Activity choice (10 minutes)

Option 1: Roll away the stone

Cut small pieces from a small foam ball to make it more rock-like. This will also make it roll funny. Create a set of tape lines on a tabletop or on the floor. Assign point values to each tape line with the highest point value the farthest from the start line.

Review the Bible story by allowing kids to answer a review question. When a kid answers a review question correctly, she may "roll away the stone" to earn points. Sample questions:

1. Who went with Jesus to pray in the garden? (*Peter, James and John—the sons of Zebedee; Matt. 26:36-37*)

2. What did the disciples do when Jesus was praying? (*slept; Matt. 26:40,43,45*)

3. Who did the crowd demand to have released? (*Barabbas, Matt. 27:21*)

4. What did the religious leaders do to prevent Jesus' body from being stolen? (*sealed the stone and had the tomb guarded, Matt. 27:62-66*)

5. When did Jesus rise from the grave? (*the first day of the week after the Sabbath, the third day; Matt. 28:1,5-6*)

6. Who told the women that Jesus was alive? (*the angel of the Lord, Matt. 28:5-6*)

7. ***What did Jesus do for sinners? Jesus' death and resurrection paid the penalty for sins and provided the promise of new life.***

8. Who made the blood sacrifice once and for all? (*Jesus made the blood sacrifice once and for all for the forgiveness of sin.*)

Say • Next week we will study what happened to Jesus' followers after His death and resurrection.

- markers
- construction or tissue paper scraps, various colors
- construction paper
- scissors
- glue
- Bible Story Picture Poster (enhanced CD)

Option 2: Modern art drawings

Guide boys and girls to recreate today's Bible story picture in a modern art style. Kids may use any combination of straight lines, circles, triangles, squares, and other geometric shapes to create the scene. Allow kids to cut the shapes and glue them to a piece of paper.

Option: Guide kids to create separate scenes from the Bible story: empty cross on Calvary, closed tomb, empty tomb, and so forth.

Help kids create a title plate for their work of modern art by cutting a small rectangle piece of construction paper. Instruct boys and girls to write on the title plate a caption or title for the picture and the artist's name. Allow kids freedom to be creative in creating their pictures.

Say • *What did Jesus do for sinners? Jesus' death and resurrection paid the penalty for sins and provided the promise of new life.*

• Your picture depicts the Easter story. Do you have a friend or family member who doesn't understand that Jesus came to pay the price for his or her sin?

This week, spend time praying for that friend or family member. Ask God to help you share the story of Jesus' death and resurrection with that person.

Journal and prayer (5 minutes)

• pencils
• journals
• Bibles
• Journal Page, 1 per kid (enhanced CD)
• "Gospel Coin Drop" activity page, 1 per kid
• coins, 1 per pair

Guide kids to write a prayer to God in response to the Bible story and big picture question. Review the big picture question.

Say • *What did Jesus do for sinners? Jesus' death and resurrection paid the penalty for sins and provided the promise of new life.*

Review Acts 4:12 and explain that knowing and loving Jesus is the only way we are forgiven. Remind kids that you are available to answer any questions they have about how to become a Christian.

As time allows, lead kids to choose a partner and play the game on the "Gospel Coin Drop" activity page.

Teacher BIBLE STUDY

Perhaps one of the most gracious things Jesus did after His resurrection was appear to the disciples, proving He was alive. The disciples were devastated to see that Jesus had died. How could He save them if He was dead? Even though Jesus had foretold His death and resurrection (Matt. 20:17-19), Jesus' disciples believed by seeing.

Jesus showed the disciples His hands and His side to prove He was not a ghost. He had a real, physical body. Then He spoke to them: "As the Father has sent Me, I also send you" (John 20:21). This verse contains the Gospel of John's version of the Great Commission. Jesus, the One sent from the Father, was now sending the disciples to be His messengers and representatives. Jesus equipped the disciples with the Holy Spirit to proclaim the gospel.

Thomas, who was not with the disciples when Jesus came, had a hard time believing that they saw Him. Thomas wanted physical proof—and that is just what He got! Jesus showed Thomas His hands and His side. Thomas immediately believed.

Jesus' resurrection proved that God was satisfied with Jesus' blood sacrifice for sins and that God's new covenant had begun. In 1 Corinthians 15, Paul addressed how the resurrection is essential to the gospel. In verse 17, Paul writes, "If Christ has not been raised, your faith is worthless; you are still in your sins."

If Christ had remained dead, His death would have meant nothing more than yours or mine. Humanity would still be without hope. Jesus' resurrection gives us hope that we one day too will be raised and changed. God gives us victory over death through Jesus. Emphasize to the kids you teach that Jesus is alive! Share with them that they have a special purpose: to tell others that Jesus is alive. He is reigning as King today over all of creation.

Older Kids BIBLE STUDY OVERVIEW

Session Title: Jesus Appeared to Many People
Bible Passage: Luke 24:36-49; John 20:19-29; Acts 1:3,9-11
Big Picture Question: What did Jesus do after He was raised from the dead? Jesus appeared to many people as proof that God had raised Jesus from the dead, and He is still alive today.
Key Passage: Luke 24:46-47
Unit Christ Connection: God's plan for redemption is fulfilled through the death and resurrection of Jesus Christ.

Small Group Opening

Large Group Leader

Small Group Leader

The BIBLE STORY

Jesus Appeared to Many People

Luke 24:36-49; John 20:19-29; Acts 1:3,9-11

On the first day of the week, in the evening, the disciples gathered together in a house. They locked the doors because they were afraid of the Jews. They didn't want to be killed like Jesus had been killed. But wait … Jesus had appeared to two disciples on the road, and Mary Magdalene had reported seeing Him alive too. Could it be true?

As the disciples talked, Jesus came, stood among them, and said to them, "Peace to you!"

The disciples were afraid! They couldn't believe their eyes! Was this really Jesus? The disciples thought they were seeing a ghost.

"Why are you afraid? It's Me! Why do you doubt?" Jesus said. "Look at Me and touch Me. A ghost does not have flesh and bones, but I do. I'm not a ghost."

Jesus showed His disciples His hands and His side. They saw the nail holes in His hands and the hole in His side. Jesus was alive? It seemed too good to be true. The disciples rejoiced because they were so happy to see Jesus!

The disciples gave Jesus some fish to eat. Jesus talked to them and explained the Bible to them. "The Bible is about Me," Jesus said. Then Jesus told them that they had a job to do. Jesus had died and was raised from the dead so that people could be forgiven for their sins. The disciples needed to tell other people to repent from their sin and be forgiven.

"Peace to you!" Jesus said to them again. "God sent Me to earth, and in the same way, I am sending you." Then Jesus breathed on them and said, "Receive the Holy Spirit." Jesus sent out the disciples to be His witnesses and to tell all the people that He is alive.

One of the disciples, Thomas, was not there when Jesus came. The other disciples kept telling him, "We have seen Jesus!" But Thomas doubted. He said, "I don't believe you! I want to see and touch the holes in His hands and His side or I will never believe!"

Eight days passed, and the disciples were indoors again. This time, Thomas was with them. Even though the doors were locked, Jesus came in and stood among them. He said, "Peace to you!"

Then He said to Thomas, "Touch the marks on My hands and My side. Don't be an unbeliever; believe!"

Thomas believed. "My Lord and my God!" he said.

Jesus said, "Because you have seen Me, you have believed. Those who believe in Me without seeing Me are blessed."

Jesus continued to appear to the disciples, proving He was alive, and He taught them about the kingdom of God.

Jesus later went up into the sky on a cloud. His disciples watched Him go into heaven. Two men appeared and told Jesus' disciples that Jesus would come back to earth one day.

Christ Connection: For 40 days, Jesus presented Himself to at least 500 people and proved that He is alive. (1 Corinthians 15:3-8) Jesus is still alive today.

Small Group OPENING

Session Title: Jesus Appeared to Many People
Bible Passage: Luke 24:36-49; John 20:19-29; Acts 1:3,9-11
Big Picture Question: What did Jesus do after He was raised from the dead? Jesus appeared to many people as proof that God had raised Jesus from the dead, and He is still alive today.
Key Passage: Luke 24:46-47
Unit Christ Connection: God's plan for redemption is fulfilled through the death and resurrection of Jesus Christ.

Welcome time

Use this time to collect the offering, fill out attendance sheets, and help new kids connect to your group. Invite kids to share something they did with their families this week. Help new kids to connect to the group by talking with them one-on-one and inviting other kids to join the conversation.

• "I Believe" activity page, 1 per kid
• pencils

Activity page (5 minutes)

Lead kids to complete the activity page, "I Believe." Ask kids to share why they answered some of the statements the way they did.

Say • It is important for us to know what we believe. It is also important for us to know *why* we believe what we believe. What is one reason you believe Jesus died and rose again?

Session starter (10 minutes)

Option 1: It's not this, it's that
Explain to kids that you will read an "it's not this, it's that" statement. The goal is for the kids to discover the pattern. Game statements:

    1. It's not a ball. It's a bee.

Tip: If the game ends early, challenge kids to name as many living things as they can in a minute. If no one mentions Jesus, remind kids of last week's Bible story.

2. It's not a glove. It's a gorilla.

3. It's not a hula hoop. It's a human.

4. It's not a TV. It's a rose.

5. It's not a dance shoe. It's a frog.

Allow three guesses after each statement. (*Answer: The pattern is that the first thing is not alive, but the second thing is alive.*)

Say • Jesus is alive! Today we will hear what happened after God raised Jesus from the dead.

• large number of items of your choice, estimate 3 items per kid
• Bibles, 1 per kid

Option: Read Matthew 28:19-20 and Acts 1:8

Option 2: Pass it on

Gather a large number of items into a pile. Items could be cotton balls, books, small toys, wads of scrap paper, and so forth. Items should be easy to pass from one kid to another.

Ask kids to stand or sit in a circle formation. Explain that you will hand items to a player one-by-one. Each item is to be passed to the right around the circle. Each item may not be put down. If a player drops an item, she must pick it up. The number of items will continue to increase. When the kids begin to struggle to keep up or begin to drop multiple items, stop the game and debrief.

Say • The gospel—the good news of Jesus' life, death and resurrection—is a message that God's people are to share with others. We are to pass it on. In our game, you had too many items to manage. It would be hard for one person to tell every non-Christian about Jesus. We *all* must share the message of Christ. It is a command Jesus gave His followers.

Guide kids to read Luke 24:46-49 and John 20:21.

Say • Today we will hear more of what Jesus told His followers after God raised Him from the dead.

Transition to large group

Large Group LEADER

Session Title: Jesus Appeared to Many People
Bible Passage: Luke 24:36-49; John 20:19-29; Acts 1:3,9-11
Big Picture Question: What did Jesus do after He was raised from the dead? Jesus appeared to many people as proof that God had raised Jesus from the dead, and He is still alive today.
Key Passage: Luke 24:46-47
Unit Christ Connection: God's plan for redemption is fulfilled through the death and resurrection of Jesus Christ.

• countdown video

Countdown

Show the countdown video as your kids arrive, and set it to end as large group time begins.

• items with a hole: a ring, paper with a hole cut out, colander, funnel, slotted spoon, and so forth

Introduce the session (2 minutes)

[Place the items in a pile at the front of the teaching area. As you begin the session, hold up each item in the pile for the kids to see.]

Leader •What is all of this stuff? Where did it come from? Did you dump all this stuff here? No, you aren't responsible. Two weeks ago we had coats and palm branches everywhere. We learned that people welcomed Jesus into Jerusalem with coats and palm branches. Last week our room was empty. We learned that Jesus died on the cross and rose from the grave. The women went to the tomb only to find out it was empty. The tomb is empty because Jesus is alive.

Our room has been connected to our Bible story each week. So what do you think? Is this pile of stuff connected to our Bible story today? Yes. You are right! How is it connected? I am not going to tell you. You have to listen to the Bible story and figure it all out.

Big picture question (1 minute)

Leader • Last week we studied Jesus' death and resurrection. Our big picture question was, ***What did Jesus do for sinners?*** The answer was, ***Jesus' death and resurrection paid the penalty for sins and provided the promise of new life.*** But what happened after all of that? What happened after the resurrection? ***What did Jesus do after He was raised from the dead?*** That is our big picture question, ***What did Jesus do after He was raised from the dead?*** Check out the timeline map to see where in the Bible we will explore today.

• Timeline Map

Timeline map (1 minute)

To help kids continue to connect the chronology of the Bible together, point out each picture on the timeline map as well as the story title on the timeline.

Leader • Here is our Bible story picture from last week, the empty tomb. And our next picture shows Jesus with some of the disciples. The timeline says part of our Bible story is in Luke, part is in John, and part of our Bible story is in the Book of Acts. In what part of the Bible is the Book of Luke located—Old or New Testament? Right, it is in the New Testament. Now does anyone know what division Luke is in? Good! Luke is located in the Gospels. The first four books of the New Testament are called the Gospels. Turn in your Bible to find the Book of Luke. The Book of John is located right after the Book of Luke. You can look it up a little later.

• "Jesus Appeared to Many People" video
• Bibles
• Bible Story Picture Slide or Poster (enhanced CD)
• Big Picture Question Slide or Poster (enhanced CD)

Tell the Bible story (10 minutes)

Open your Bible to Luke 24 and tell the Bible story in your own words, or show the Bible story video "Jesus Appeared to Many People."

Leader • What is the answer to our big picture question? *What did Jesus do after He was raised from the dead?* You were really listening to our Bible story! *Jesus appeared to many people as proof that God had raised Jesus from the dead, and He is still alive today.* Where were the disciples when Jesus appeared to them? Yes! They were in a locked room. They were afraid. What did Jesus say when He appeared? He told them "Peace to you." That was a common greeting used by the Jewish people. But peace is also a blessing or gift that Christians have because Jesus is alive. He paid the penalty for our sin and defeated evil through His death and resurrection. Followers of Jesus don't have to be afraid. We can have peace because we know Jesus is the all-powerful, risen Lord and Savior.

Jesus explained to the disciples that Scripture told about Him. Everything the Scriptures said about Jesus had happened or would one day happen. Jesus also told the disciples to go and tell people about Him. Jesus told them to share with people that He had died and was resurrected so people could repent of their sins and be forgiven.

Thomas didn't believe that Jesus was alive because he did not see Jesus. Thomas wanted proof. He wanted to see and touch the holes in Jesus' hands and His side. Do you ever want proof before you believe something? Sometimes we do. Thomas wanted to see Jesus was alive before he chose to believe what the disciples told him. Jesus loves us and He graciously helps us when we truly need it. Jesus knew that Thomas needed to see Him, so He appeared to Thomas. When Thomas saw Jesus, Thomas called Jesus two special names. Does anyone remember which two names? Thomas called Jesus his Lord and his God. He believed that Jesus was alive! Jesus told Thomas that people who believe in Him without seeing Him are blessed.

Jesus appeared to at least 500 people in the 40 days after His resurrection. Do you know what those people did? They went and told others about Jesus. And those people told others about Jesus. Now it is our mission to tell others about Jesus.

What did Jesus do after He was raised from the dead? Jesus appeared to many people as proof that God had raised Jesus from the dead, and He is still alive today.

Key passage (4 minutes)

• Key Passage Slide or Poster (enhanced CD)
• "Luke 24:46-47" song

Leader •Our key passage was a part of our Bible story. With how many nations are we to share the message about Jesus? What does our key passage say? Our key passage says we must share the gospel of Jesus with *all* nations. Do I have a volunteer who can quote the key passage from memory?

If you have a volunteer, allow her to quote the key passage. Lead all the kids to read the key passage together. Sing "Luke 24:46-47."

• "Jesus Saves" song

Sing (5 minutes)

Leader •Let's praise Jesus for being our risen Lord and Savior. He is worthy of our praise. We have so much to praise Him for. Tell me one thing we can praise Jesus for. Allow several kids to respond.

Leader •All of those are great reasons to praise Jesus. Our key passage reminds us to share the message about Jesus. We can share that message by singing our theme song. Sing "Jesus Saves."

Discussion starter video (5 minutes)

• "Unit 7 Session 3" discussion starter video

Leader • Sometimes it is hard to believe without proof. I can understand how Thomas felt. Has someone ever told you something and you weren't sure you should believe it? Check out this video.

Show the "Unit 7 Session 3" discussion starter video.

Leader • What do you think? What would you have done if you were Thomas? Would you have believed the other disciples, or would you have wanted to see proof?

The Gospel: God's Plan for Me (optional)

• Bible

Leader • Some people don't believe Jesus is their Lord and God as Thomas did. God planned from the beginning to send Jesus to die on the cross for our sin and to raise Him from the grave. God created the way for us to be forgiven.

Review the gospel plan using the guide provided.

Prayer (2 minutes)

Leader • Did anyone guess what all the items in the pile tell us about today's Bible story? I'll give you a clue. All the items have one thing in common. Yes! All the items have a hole. What does a hole have to do with today's Bible story? Great answer! Thomas insisted he had to see and touch the holes in Jesus' hands and side. He wanted proof before He would believe Jesus is alive.

What did Jesus do after He was raised from the dead? Jesus appeared to many people as proof that God had raised Jesus from the dead, and He is still alive today.

Join me in prayer and praise God for raising Jesus from the dead.

Close in prayer.

Dismiss to small groups

The Gospel: God's Plan for Me

Ask kids if they have ever heard the word *gospel*. Clarify that the word *gospel* means "good news." It is the message about Christ, the kingdom of God, and salvation. Use the following guide to share the gospel with kids.

God rules. Explain to kids that the Bible tells us God created everything, and He is in charge of everything. Invite a volunteer to read Genesis 1:1 from the Bible. Read Revelation 4:11 or Colossians 1:16-17 aloud and explain what these verses mean.

We sinned. Tell kids that since the time of Adam and Eve, everyone has chosen to disobey God. (Romans 3:23) The Bible calls this sin. Because God is holy, God cannot be around sin. Sin separates us from God and deserves God's punishment of death. (Romans 6:23)

God provided. Choose a child to read John 3:16 aloud. Say that God sent His Son, Jesus, the perfect solution to our sin problem, to rescue us from the punishment we deserve. It's something we, as sinners, could never earn on our own. Jesus alone saves us. Read and explain Ephesians 2:8-9.

Jesus gives. Share with kids that Jesus lived a perfect life, died on the cross for our sins, and rose again. Because Jesus gave up His life for us, we can be welcomed into God's family for eternity. This is the best gift ever! Read Romans 5:8; 2 Corinthians 5:21; or 1 Peter 3:18.

We respond. Tell kids that they can respond to Jesus. Read Romans 10:9-10,13. Review these aspects of our response: Believe in your heart that Jesus alone saves you through what He's already done on the cross. Repent, turning from self and sin to Jesus. Tell God and others that your faith is in Jesus.

Offer to talk with any child who is interested in responding to Jesus.

Small Group LEADER

Session Title: Jesus Appeared to Many People
Bible Passage: Luke 24:36-49; John 20:19-29; Acts 1:3,9-11
Big Picture Question: What did Jesus do after He was raised from the dead? Jesus appeared to many people as proof that God had raised Jesus from the dead, and He is still alive today.
Key Passage: Luke 24:46-47
Unit Christ Connection: God's plan for redemption is fulfilled through the death and resurrection of Jesus Christ.

Bible story review & Bible skills (10 minutes)

- Bibles, 1 per kid
- Small Group Visual Pack
- sticky notes or tabs

To continue helping kids build confidence about reading Scripture aloud, invite kids to take turns reading a verse of today's Bible story from John 20. Complete the reading by reading Acts 1:3 to the kids. Ask the boys and girls what they would have felt if they were Thomas. Would they have believed, or would they want to see Jesus before believing?

Say • *What did Jesus do after He was raised from the dead? Jesus appeared to many people as proof that God had raised Jesus from the dead, and He is still alive today.*

• How many people saw Jesus alive after His resurrection? (*For 40 days, Jesus presented Himself to at least 500 people and proved that He is alive. [1 Corinthians 15:3-8] Jesus is still alive today.*)

You may opt to review how to become a Christian using the guide provided. Explain to kids that if they have any questions or need to talk with someone that they should let you or another teacher know. They may also choose to talk with their parents after class. If time allows, guide kids to locate some of the Scriptures in their Bibles. Lead kids to mark the verses with a sticky note or tab.

- **God rules.** God created and is in charge of everything. (Gen. 1:1; Rev. 4:11; Col. 1:16-17)
- **We sinned.** Since Adam and Eve, everyone has chosen to disobey God. (Rom. 3:23; 6:23)
- **God provided.** God sent His Son Jesus to rescue us from the punishment we deserve. (John 3:16; Eph. 2:8-9)
- **Jesus gives.** Jesus lived a perfect life, died on the cross for our sins, and rose again so we can be welcomed into God's family. (Rom. 5:8; 2 Cor. 5:21; 1 Pet. 3:18)
- **We respond.** Believe that Jesus alone saves you. Repent. Tell God that your faith is in Jesus. (Rom. 10:9-10,13)

Key passage activity (5 minutes)

• Key Passage Poster (enhanced CD)

Form pairs or trios. Guide kids to open their Bibles and locate the unit key passage, Luke 24:46-47. Each kid should read one of the verses from his Bible, close his Bible, and try to say the verse from memory. If he can't say it from memory, he may reopen his Bible and read the verse again. Once he says one verse from memory, he should try to add the second verse.

Say • Jesus wanted His disciples to tell people from all nations about Him. This key passage is a command for all believers. We are to tell people about Jesus too.

Activity choice (10 minutes)

Option 1: Looking for proof game

Invite kids to form a circle. Explain that everyone will close their eyes and you will tap one kid on the back. You will ask everyone to open their eyes. The kid you tapped will begin to secretly wink or smile at other kids.

Explain that when a player sees someone wink or smile at her, she must count silently to three and say, "Jesus is alive" to notify everyone she is out. The player may not give away who winked or smiled. Kids should deduce who is winking or smiling by watching for clues to prove who it is without getting "out." When a kid thinks she knows who it is, she must say "peace to you" and reveal her guess and what proof she thinks she has. A wrong guess is out. A correct guess ends the round and the game begins again.

Say • *What did Jesus do after He was raised from the dead? Jesus appeared to many people as proof that God had raised Jesus from the dead, and He is still alive today.*

- Jesus appeared to many people to help them understand He is alive. He proved He had defeated sin and death through His resurrection.
- We can believe Jesus died for our sins and was resurrected or we can choose not to believe. Like Thomas, we can choose whether or not we believe without seeing. We can chose to believe without seeing and be blessed as Jesus said.
- How many people saw Jesus alive after His resurrection? (*For 40 days, Jesus presented Himself to at least 500 people and proved that He is alive. [1 Corinthians 15:3-8] Jesus is still alive today.*)

- round paper metal rim key tags, white
- fine point permanent markers
- small stickers (optional)

Option 2: "I believe" key tag

Help kids create a key tag using permanent markers and any other decorating items you provided. Suggest kids print the phrase *I believe. John 20:29* or *Peace be with you. John 20:26* or another phrase from today's Bible story on the key tag. Kids may decorate their tags as time allows.

Say • Where were the disciples when Jesus appeared to

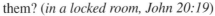

them? (*in a locked room, John 20:19*)

- When Jesus appeared inside a locked room, it was another sign of His power. He had risen from the grave. He is all-powerful. When you look at your key tag, remember that Jesus is all-powerful. Nothing—not even a locked door—could prevent Jesus from following God's plan. Nothing should stop us from obeying God's plan.

- *What did Jesus do after He was raised from the dead? Jesus appeared to many people as proof that God had raised Jesus from the dead, and He is still alive today.*

- How many people saw Jesus alive after His resurrection? (*For 40 days, Jesus presented Himself to at least 500 people and proved that He is alive. [1 Corinthians 15:3-8] Jesus is still alive today.*)

Journal and prayer (5 minutes)

- pencils
- journals
- Bibles
- Journal Page, 1 per kid (enhanced CD)
- "Eyewitness Maze" activity page, 1 per kid

Guide kids to write a prayer about why they do or don't believe Jesus is alive. Remind kids that you will not read their prayers unless they ask you to.

Say • *What did Jesus do after He was raised from the dead? Jesus appeared to many people as proof that God had raised Jesus from the dead, and He is still alive today.*

Pray for all the kids in your group to believe that God sent Jesus to die for their sins and that God raised Jesus from the dead. Pray for kids to have boldness to share with others the truth about Jesus.

As time allows, help kids locate 1 Corinthians 15:3-8 in the Bible. Lead kids to complete the "Eyewitness Maze" activity page.

Unit 8: JOSHUA

Big Picture Questions

Session 1: What should God's people remember? God's people should remember how He has saved and sustained them.

Session 2: Who fought the battle of Jericho? God fought for His people and handed Jericho over to the Israelites.

Session 3: How does God feel about sin? God hates sin and punishes sin.

Session 4: What does God do when we obey Him? God blesses people who obey Him in faith.

Session 5: What does God do when we pray? God answers the prayers of His people and saves them.

Session 6: How can we show we love God? We can serve, worship, and obey God.

Unit 8: JOSHUA

Unit Description: Joshua was Moses' successor. Because of his
faithfulness to God in the wilderness, Joshua was chosen to lead
God's people into the land God had promised to Abraham. Again, God
supernaturally enabled the people to enter the land and to conquer the
people who lived in it.

Unit Key Passage: Joshua 24:15

Unit Christ Connection: Joshua was a representation of Christ, leading
the Israelites to victory in overcoming Canaan as Jesus leads us to
victory in overcoming the world.

Session 1: The Israelites Crossed the Jordan River
Joshua 3–4

Session 2: The Conquest of Jericho
Joshua 2; 6

Session 3: Achan Sinned
Joshua 7

Session 4: The Defeat of Ai
Joshua 8

Session 5: The Day the Sun Stood Still
Joshua 10:1-15

Session 6: Joshua's Final Encouragement
Joshua 23:1–24:28

Teacher BIBLE STUDY

Only one geographical barrier separated the Israelites from the promised land of Canaan: the Jordan River. When Joshua and the Israelites arrived, the Jordan River was flooded due to spring rains and snowmelt. Any other time, the river would have been manageable, but crossing the swollen river would have been as daunting as crossing the Red Sea. (See Josh. 4:23.)

God gave Joshua a promise and a command. First, He promised to drive out from before them all the people of the land. Then God told him to tell the priests to carry the ark of the LORD (a symbol of God's powerful presence) into the waters of the Jordan. Then the waters of the river would be cut off from flowing, and the waters coming down from above would stand in one heap.

The priests did as Joshua commanded. The waters stopped, and all of the people passed over on dry ground. The LORD commanded Joshua to have 12 men each take a stone from the middle of the Jordan. When the priests came up out of the river, the water started to flow and was again flooded. Joshua set up the stones to be a memorial. The stones served as a reminder of God's faithfulness in bringing Israel safely across the Jordan into the promised land.

The Israelites could do nothing apart from God. He was with them, and He was going to fight for them. In John 15:5, Jesus said, "You can do nothing without Me." As you teach kids this week, emphasize that God was just getting started. He was going to do even bigger things for the Israelites— saving them from their enemies and one day sending them a Savior. The cross is our reminder of what Jesus has done for us: a miraculous saving we could never do for ourselves.

Older Kids BIBLE STUDY OVERVIEW

Session Title: The Israelites Crossed the Jordan River
Bible Passage: Joshua 3–4
Big Picture Question: What should God's people remember? God's people should remember how He has saved and sustained them.
Key Passage: Joshua 24:15
Unit Christ Connection: Joshua was a representation of Christ, leading the Israelites to victory in overcoming Canaan as Jesus leads us to victory in overcoming the world.

Small Group Opening

Large Group Leader

Small Group Leader

The BIBLE STORY

The Israelites Crossed the Jordan River
Joshua 3–4

Moses had died, and God told Joshua to be in charge of the Israelites. God said that it was time for them to enter the promised land. So Joshua got up early the next morning and the Israelites traveled toward the Jordan River, which separated them from the promised land, the land of Canaan (KAY nuhn). They camped next to the river for three days.

Then the officers told everyone that it was almost time to cross the river. They gave the people instructions: "Set out when you see the priests carrying the ark of the covenant. Make yourselves clean; God is going to do great things tomorrow."

God said to Joshua, "I am going to lift you up as the leader so the people will know that you are going to lead them like Moses did." God told Joshua to command the priests carrying the ark to stand in the water at the edge of the Jordan River. Joshua told all of the Israelites to come close and listen.

"God is here with us," Joshua said. "He will defeat our enemies for us. When the priests carrying the ark of the covenant stand in the river, the water will stop." The priests moved into the river and the water stopped and stood up on one side. All of the people crossed the Jordan on dry ground.

After everyone had crossed, God told Joshua to choose one man from each of the 12 tribes of Israel. Each man was to take a stone from the middle of the river and set it down where the Israelites would spend the night. Now the priests carrying the ark of the covenant crossed the river. The water started to flow again.

The people camped at a city called Gilgal (GIL gal) on the east side of Jericho (JER ih koh). Joshua set up the 12 stones they had taken from the Jordan and he said to the Israelites, "In the future, when your children ask their fathers, 'What is the meaning of these stones?' you should tell your children, 'Israel crossed the Jordan on dry ground.' For the LORD your God dried up the waters of the Jordan before you until you had crossed over, just as the LORD your God did to the Red Sea. This is so all the people of the earth may know that the LORD's hand is mighty, and so that you may always fear the LORD your God."

Christ Connection: God told Joshua and the Israelites to set up memorial stones to remember what God had done to bring them into the promised land. On the night He died, Jesus told His disciples to remember the sacrifice He was going to make to save us from our sins. When Christians take the Lord's Supper, they remember God's plan to destroy sin through Jesus' death and resurrection. (1 Corinthians 11:26)

Small Group OPENING

Session Title: The Israelites Crossed the Jordan River
Bible Passage: Joshua 3–4
Big Picture Question: What should God's people remember? God's people should remember how He has saved and sustained them.
Key Passage: Joshua 24:15
Unit Christ Connection: Joshua was a representation of Christ, leading the Israelites to victory in overcoming Canaan as Jesus leads us to victory in overcoming the world.

Welcome time

• journals

Greet each kid as he or she arrives. Use this time to collect the offering, fill out attendance sheets, and help new kids connect to your group. Allow boys and girls to look at their journals and share any prayer requests that God has answered.

Activity page (5 minutes)

• "Rock Memories" activity page, 1 per kid
• pencils

Guide kids to complete the activity page, "Rock Memories."

Say •Good memories are wonderful. In the Bible, people often built memorials to help them remember what God had done or said to them. The Israelites had a great day in today's Bible story. God wanted them to remember what they learned.

Session starter (10 minutes)

Option 1: Across the river relay

• construction paper or felt

Create boundary markers on each side of the room to represent the two river banks. Form two teams and provide one member of each team with two pieces of construction paper. The first player on each team must place one piece of construction paper down, step on it, place the second piece

Tip: To help prevent slipping on carpet, provide pieces of felt.

To avoid slipping on tile flooring, consider playing with pieces of non-skid rug backing.

of paper down, and then step on it. He should grab the first piece of paper, place it in front of the second piece of paper and move forward.

The player must continue the pattern, stepping only on the paper, until he is across the river (the room). He must then "swim" (move arms in swimming motion while walking) back to his team with the two pieces of paper and hand them to the next person. Continue until every kid has crossed the river and returned.

Say • Great work. In today's Bible story the Israelites faced a challenge. The Jordan River was flooded, but the Israelites needed to get across so they could conquer the promised land. Listen closely to discover how they crossed the river.

Option 2: Floating vessel

Guide kids to create a vessel to float a coin in a bowl of water. Each vessel must use more than one of the supplied objects. Allow kids about seven minutes to create a vessel. Lead kids to take turns testing the vessel in the bowl of water.

• drinking straws
• craft sticks
• sponges
• masking tape
• markers
• index cards
• coins or buttons, 1 per vessel
• large bowl or pan of water

Tip: If kids are not sure where to start, encourage them to try using the drinking straws and tape.

Say • Great work. In today's Bible story the Israelites faced a challenge. The Jordan River was flooded, but the Israelites needed to get across so they could conquer the promised land. Floating across the river was not a good option. Swimming across the river was not a good idea. Listen closely to discover how they crossed the river.

Transition to large group

Large Group LEADER

Session Title: The Israelites Crossed the Jordan River
Bible Passage: Joshua 3–4
Big Picture Question: What should God's people remember? God's people should remember how He has saved and sustained them.
Key Passage: Joshua 24:15
Unit Christ Connection: Joshua was a representation of Christ, leading the Israelites to victory in overcoming Canaan as Jesus leads us to victory in overcoming the world.

• room decorations

Tip: Decorate as much or as little as your space and budget allow.

Suggested Theme Decorating Ideas: Create flags or banners similar in style to ones soldiers once carried into battle. Stack old building stones in small piles around the teaching area. You may wish to hang a gray backdrop to represent a stone fort wall. Or hang brick, stone, or wood patterned paper to form a fort wall. You may cut large cardboard or foam board pieces to resemble the top of a fort wall. You could also cut windows into the cardboard.

• countdown video

Countdown

Show the countdown video as your kids arrive, and set it to end as large group time begins.

Introduce the session (2 minutes)

[Large Group Leader enters, marching.]

Leader • Left, left, left, right, left. Left, left, left, right, left. Oh, hi, everybody! It's good to see you. I'm practicing my marching because this week we are at the remains of an old fort. Did you know we are at a fort? Forts were usually built to protect people. People don't really build forts anymore. Back when they did build forts, they were usually used by soldiers. Soldiers stayed in forts to protect people and the land. One of the things soldiers do is march. They march from one spot to another. They march instead of just walking. It helps keep everyone in the right spot and moving in a nice orderly way.

We need to practice our marching. Everyone stand up. You aren't going to move from your spot. You are going to march in place when I give the command. Every time I say the word *right* or the word *left* you take a step. Ready, is everyone ready?

Left, left, left, right, left. Left, left, left, right, left. Once more. Left, left, left, right, left. Left, left, left, right, left. I see some people who might become great soldiers one day. OK, everyone take a seat.

• Timeline Map

Timeline map (1 minute)

Leader •The Israelites have had quite a journey so far. When I give you the signal, shout out one thing that has happened to Moses and the Israelites.

Point to three to five kids and allow them to respond.

Leader •Great answers, everyone! We know we are at a fort, but do we know what our Bible story is or our big picture question?

According to our timeline, today's Bible story is "The Israelites Crossed the Jordan River." The Bible story is found in the Book of Joshua. Where is the Book of Joshua located in the Bible? Joshua is one of the 12 books of History in the Old Testament.

Anyone want to guess why the books of History are called the books of History? The books tell the history of the Israelites. During our time at the fort, we are going to look at the history of the Israelites and their journey after the death of Moses.

Big picture question (1 minute)

Leader • Our big picture question is, ***What should God's people remember?*** What is something you think God wants you to remember?

Open your Bible to Joshua 3 and we'll discover the answer to our big picture question.

Tell the Bible story (9 minutes)

- "The Israelites Crossed the Jordan River" video
- Bibles
- Bible Story Picture Slide or Poster (enhanced CD)
- Big Picture Question Slide or Poster (enhanced CD)

Open your Bible to Joshua 3 and tell the Bible story in your own words, or show the Bible story video "The Israelites Crossed the Jordan River."

Leader • The Israelites faced a big dilemma. In order to conquer the promised land, they had to cross the Jordan River. But the river was flooded, and a lot of Israelites had to cross. On their own, the Israelites could not cross, but with God's help they did.

Why did God tell the Israelites to build a memorial? He wanted them to remember what He had done for them. He wanted it to be a sign for future generations. God wanted His people to tell their children about Him.

Our big picture question is, ***What should God's people remember?*** The answer to our big picture question is, ***God's people should remember how He has saved and sustained them.*** To *sustain* means "to support or provide." Name some of the ways God saved and sustained the Israelites so far. Great answers! God saved and sustained the Israelites many times. As we continue our chronological study through God's Word, we will hear many more stories of how God saved and sustained the Israelites.

What are some ways God has saved or sustained you? Every day God continues to save and sustain us by providing for our needs. He also sustains our salvation.

When we trust in Jesus, God saves us. He continues to hold us in His hands, and He will never let go.

• Bible

The Gospel : God's Plan for Me (optional)

Leader • The main way God has saved us is through His Son, Jesus Christ. God sent Jesus to earth to be our Savior.

Use the guide provided to explain to kids how to become a Christian. Provide kids with an opportunity to speak with a counselor in a one-on-one conversation. Encourage counselors to ask open-ended questions and allow each kid's responses and questions to guide the conversation.

• Key Passage Slide or Poster (enhanced CD)
• "Choose for Yourself" song

Key passage (5 minutes)

Leader • Our key passage is a reminder of the choice the Israelites had about whom to follow. One of the reasons God wanted the Israelites to conquer the promised land was that He wanted the Israelites to get rid of the idols or false gods the Canaanite people worshiped. God didn't want the Israelites to be around people who worshiped other gods because He knew they would not be able to resist the temptation to worship false gods. They needed to follow God and obey His instructions.

Read the key passage together. Sing "Choose for Yourself."

• "Unit 8 Session 1" discussion starter video

Discussion starter video (5 minutes)

Leader • Why do you think God wanted the Israelites to remember what He had done to save and sustain them? Do you think God wants you to remember what He has done to save and sustain you? Check out this video.

Show the "Unit 8 Session 1" discussion starter video.

Leader • Do you ever have trouble remembering things? What about the things God has done for you? Do you have trouble remembering those? Do you ever take time to sit down and list all of the things God has done for you? Why or why not? Should we? Does it help us remember what God has done to save and sustain us? Help kids connect to the big picture question as they formulate their answers.

Sing (5 minutes)

• "Our God" song

Leader • Our God is great and mighty. His power can stop a river. The Israelites remembered the mighty power of God by building a memorial. ***God's people should remember how He has saved and sustained them.*** One way we can remember how God has saved and sustained us is by singing. Our theme song is called "Our God." Lead kids in singing the unit theme song, "Our God."

Prayer (2 minutes)

Leader • *What should God's people remember? God's people should remember how He has saved and sustained them.* OK, let's try saying our big picture question as we march. Everyone stand up. Follow my commands. Left, left, left, right, left. Keep marching and say the big picture question and answer with me. *What should God's people remember? God's people should remember how He has saved and sustained them.*

Excellent job, troops! You may sit back down. I am going to end our time together by praying that we will remember how God saves and sustains us. After I pray, watch your small group leader for the signal to march to your small group.

Close in prayer.

Dismiss to small groups

The Gospel: God's Plan for Me

Ask kids if they have ever heard the word *gospel*. Clarify that the word *gospel* means "good news." It is the message about Christ, the kingdom of God, and salvation. Use the following guide to share the gospel with kids.

God rules. Explain to kids that the Bible tells us God created everything, and He is in charge of everything. Invite a volunteer to read Genesis 1:1 from the Bible. Read Revelation 4:11 or Colossians 1:16-17 aloud and explain what these verses mean.

We sinned. Tell kids that since the time of Adam and Eve, everyone has chosen to disobey God. (Romans 3:23) The Bible calls this sin. Because God is holy, God cannot be around sin. Sin separates us from God and deserves God's punishment of death. (Romans 6:23)

God provided. Choose a child to read John 3:16 aloud. Say that God sent His Son, Jesus, the perfect solution to our sin problem, to rescue us from the punishment we deserve. It's something we, as sinners, could never earn on our own. Jesus alone saves us. Read and explain Ephesians 2:8-9.

Jesus gives. Share with kids that Jesus lived a perfect life, died on the cross for our sins, and rose again. Because Jesus gave up His life for us, we can be welcomed into God's family for eternity. This is the best gift ever! Read Romans 5:8; 2 Corinthians 5:21; or 1 Peter 3:18.

We respond. Tell kids that they can respond to Jesus. Read Romans 10:9-10,13. Review these aspects of our response: Believe in your heart that Jesus alone saves you through what He's already done on the cross. Repent, turning from self and sin to Jesus. Tell God and others that your faith is in Jesus.

Offer to talk with any child who is interested in responding to Jesus.

Small Group LEADER

Session Title: The Israelites Crossed the Jordan River
Bible Passage: Joshua 3–4
Big Picture Question: What should God's people remember? God's people should remember how He has saved and sustained them.
Key Passage: Joshua 24:15
Unit Christ Connection: Joshua was a representation of Christ, leading the Israelites to victory in overcoming Canaan as Jesus leads us to victory in overcoming the world.

- Bibles, 1 per kid
- Small Group Visual Pack
- various props including blue fabric, stones, cardboard box (optional)

Option: Show kids a storying cloth scarf that is used by missionaries to share the gospel. Storying cloths are available at *www.imbresources.org.*

Bible story review & Bible skills (10 minutes)

Review the timeline in the small group visual pack to help kids see the journey of the Israelites from Egypt to today's Bible story.

Allow kids to use the method called "storying" to share the Bible story today. Ask kids to pretend they are sharing the story with someone who speaks another language.

Ask kids to select a narrator, write a few brief lines, and assign acting parts. You may provide blue fabric, stones, a box for the ark of the covenant, and other props.

Say • Storying is one way we can remember how God saved and sustained the Israelites. Missionaries use storying to share about God and the Bible with people who speak other languages. Sometimes the people may not be able to read, so it's important that we know how to tell them the stories of the Bible. No matter what method you choose, all Christians should share about God, Jesus, and the Bible with others.

- *What should God's people remember? God's people should remember how He has saved and sustained them.*

- What event do Christians participate in to remember

Tip: You may need
to pause and
explain the Lord's
Supper if you have
kids who have
not participated
in or observed the
ordinance.

Jesus' death and resurrection? (*When Christians take the Lord's Supper, they remember God's plan to destroy sin through Jesus' death and resurrection. {1 Corinthians 11:26}*)

You may opt to review how to become a Christian or allow kids to practice sharing with a partner how to become a Christian.

- **God rules.** God created and is in charge of everything. (Gen. 1:1; Rev. 4:11; Col. 1:16-17)

- **We sinned.** Since Adam and Eve, everyone has chosen to disobey God. (Rom. 3:23; 6:23)

- **God provided.** God sent His Son Jesus to rescue us from the punishment we deserve. (John 3:16; Eph. 2:8-9)

- **Jesus gives.** Jesus lived a perfect life, died on the cross for our sins, and rose again so we can be welcomed into God's family. (Rom. 5:8; 2 Cor. 5:21; 1 Pet. 3:18)

- **We respond.** Believe that Jesus alone saves you. Repent. Tell God that your faith is in Jesus. (Rom. 10:9-10,13)

Key passage activity (5 minutes)

- stones, 24
- bowls of water, 2
- towels
- permanent marker
- Key Passage Poster (enhanced CD)

Option: Cut stones from foam sheets or laminate paper stones prior to placing in water.

Write the key passage on 12 stones. Create two sets. Form two groups. Drop each team's stones in its bowl of water. At your signal, kids must take turns "fishing" out one of their team's stones. Once all 12 stones have been gathered, teams must arrange the key passage in order. Allow kids to use their Bibles to look up the key passage to help arrange the words in order.

Say • We also have a choice of whom we will follow and worship. We can worship God, or we can worship something or someone else. Why do you think people choose to worship or follow something or someone other than God?

Allow kids to respond. Encourage kids that although following God is not easy, God's plans are always perfect.

- paper bags, 12 per team
- markers
- scrap paper
- tape

Option: Ask each kid to write on a specific bag.

Activity choice (10 minutes)

Option 1: Build a memorial game

Explain that the group will build a memorial using paper bags and scrap paper. Prior to the game, allow teams to work together to write on each paper bag a way God has protected, saved, or sustained them. When finished, lead kids to stuff each paper bag with scrap paper and fold over the edges to look like a stone or rock.

Form two lines. Line up groups approximately five feet apart. Allow teams to race to pass each stone from the back to the front of their line to assemble a memorial. Once all the stones are at the front of the line, allow teams to use tape to assemble the "stones" to form a standing memorial.

Say • Is it hard to remember how God has saved and sustained you?

- *What should God's people remember? God's people should remember how He has saved and sustained them.*

- What event do Christians participate in to remember Jesus' death and resurrection? (*When Christians take the Lord's Supper, they remember God's plan to destroy sin through Jesus' death and resurrection. [1 Corinthians 11:26]*)

- scissors
- large decorative glass gemstones
- blank index cards
- markers
- dries-clear glue sticks
- pencils
- round magnets

Option 2: Memorial magnets

Tell kids to think about a time God did something in their lives. (salvation, baptism, trip to church camp, healing for a sick family member) This is a time God protected, saved,

A.

B.

C.

D.

E.

- pencils
- journals
- Bibles
- Journal Page, 1 per kid (enhanced CD)
- "Road Stops" activity page, 1 per kid

or sustained them. Ask kids to think about how they can describe that event or time in two or three words.

Lead kids to follow these steps to make a memorial stone magnet. Place a glass gemstone on an index card. Trace around the stone with a pencil. Use markers to write inside the traced circle the key words that describe the event he thought about. Cut out the circle. Spread glue over the circle and place the stone on top of the glued circle. Push together the index card circle and gemstone to help the glue connect. Allow the glue to dry for a minute or two. Glue the magnet to the paper-backed gemstone. Kids may make more than one memorial magnet if enough supplies remain.

Say • God told the Israelites to build a memorial to help them remember what He did for them. It is easy for people to forget how God has saved and sustained them. Place your magnet on your refrigerator, locker, or another place where you will see it often and remember how God has saved and sustained you.

What should God's people remember? God's people should remember how He has saved and sustained them.

Journal and prayer (5 minutes)

Invite kids to write a prayer of thanksgiving about how God has saved and sustained them. Any kid who does not want to write may draw images symbolizing the ways God has saved and sustained him.

Say • *What should God's people remember? God's people should remember how He has saved and sustained them.*

As time allows, lead kids to use the Bible to complete the activity page, "Road Stops."

Teacher BIBLE STUDY

The Lord brought His people into the promised land. Now they had a task set before them: conquer the people living in the land. The first city the Israelites came to was Jericho. The people of Jericho had heard about God and what He had done for the Israelites. They understood God's power and wanted nothing to do with Him.

Joshua sent spies to Jericho to check it out. A prostitute named Rahab knew how powerful God was. She wanted to be on God's side. Rahab hid the spies and kept them safe from the people of Jericho. In return, the spies promised that Rahab and her family would be safe when the Israelites conquered the city.

The people of Jericho worshiped false gods, and God was bringing His judgment against them. The Lord's reputation went ahead of the Israelites, creating fear in the people of Jericho. God was in control. He told Joshua that the battle would be just fine. (See Josh. 6:2.)

The battle of Jericho was fought by faith. The Israelites did not focus on what was going on inside the city of Jericho; they focused on doing what God had instructed. They obeyed even when it seemed nothing was happening. On the seventh day, the trumpets sounded, declaring, "The LORD is near!"

Joshua gave the people specific instructions to destroy everything in the city except for Rahab and her family. The Israelites were not to keep anything for themselves. The Lord was going to provide for all of their needs. They had no reason to plunder Jericho.

Jesus spoke of the Lord's provision in Matthew 6:33. As you teach kids this week, lead them to trust God for all of their needs, including their greatest need—to be rescued from sin by Jesus Christ.

Unit 8 • Session 2
© 2012 LifeWay Christian Resources

Older Kids BIBLE STUDY OVERVIEW

Session Title: The Conquest of Jericho
Bible Passage: Joshua 2; 6
Big Picture Question: Who fought the battle of Jericho? God fought for His people and handed Jericho over to the Israelites.
Key Passage: Joshua 24:15
Unit Christ Connection: Joshua was a representation of Christ, leading the Israelites to victory in overcoming Canaan as Jesus leads us to victory in overcoming the world.

Small Group Opening

Large Group Leader

Small Group Leader

The BIBLE STORY

The Conquest of Jericho
Joshua 2; 6

The Israelites were camping near the Jordan River. The Israelites were so close to the land God had promised to give them! There was one more thing they had to do: take it over. Many other people lived in Canaan (KAY nuhn), and the Israelites had to defeat them.

Joshua sent two spies into Jericho to check it out. They stayed at the house of a woman named Rahab (RAY hab). The king of Jericho heard the spies were with Rahab, so Rahab hid the men on her roof to keep them safe. Rahab had heard what God did to Pharaoh and believed in God. She wanted to help His people. When it was safe for the spies to leave, Rahab said, "Please be kind to my family since we have been kind to you. When you attack Jericho, please do not kill us." So the spies promised to keep Rahab and her family safe, and they left Jericho. Rahab tied a bright red rope in her window so the Israelites would know which house she lived in.

Now the city of Jericho was closed up—no one left, and no one entered in. The people in Jericho knew the Israelites were near. They hid behind the walls of the city. God said to Joshua, "Jericho is yours. You will conquer it. Here is what you should do: March around the city one time each day for six days. On the seventh day, march around the city seven times, and the priests should blow the trumpets. Then all the people should shout, and the walls of Jericho will fall down. The Israelites can then go into the city and conquer it."

Just as God said, Joshua commanded the people to carry the ark of the covenant and march around the city. The priests blew their trumpets. They marched around the city one time. Not one of the Israelites spoke or made a sound, just like Joshua commanded them. The second day, they silently marched around the city again and then returned to their camp. They did this every day for six days.

On the seventh day, the Israelites got up early and marched around the city seven times. On the seventh time when the priests blew their trumpets, Joshua said, "Shout, for the LORD has given you the city!" So the people shouted, and the wall fell down flat so that the Israelites went into the city and captured it. They destroyed everything in the city, keeping none of it for themselves.

The two spies spared a woman named Rahab (RAY hab) and her family, who had hidden them when they were spies in the land. Rahab was saved because of her faith in God. Joshua declared, "Anyone who tries to rebuild this city will be cursed."

God was with Joshua, and everyone in the land knew of Joshua and what he had done.

Christ Connection: God gave the city of Jericho to the Israelites. He fought the battle for them and told them not to take anything from the city. God promised to provide for His people's needs. Jesus spoke of God's provision in Matthew 6:33, "Seek first the kingdom of God and His righteousness, and all these things will be provided for you." Jesus meets our greatest need—to be saved from our sin. We can trust Him for our salvation.

Small Group OPENING

Session Title: The Conquest of Jericho
Bible Passage: Joshua 2; 6
Big Picture Question: Who fought the battle of Jericho? God fought for His people and handed Jericho over to the Israelites.
Key Passage: Joshua 24:15
Unit Christ Connection: Joshua was a representation of Christ, leading the Israelites to victory in overcoming Canaan as Jesus leads us to victory in overcoming the world.

Welcome time

Greet kids. Use this time to collect the offering, fill out attendance sheets, and help new kids connect to your group. Invite kids to share the highlights of their week.

Activity page (5 minutes)

- "Time Race" activity page, 1 per kid
- pencils
- stopwatch or timer
- Bibles, 1 per kid

Distribute the "Time Race" activity page facedown. Tell kids that when you give the command to start, they may turn over the activity sheet and follow the instructions. Time kids to see who correctly completes the activity page first.

Say • How many of you followed the instructions at the top of the page? Was it important to follow the instructions? The Israelites faced a big battle in today's Bible story. God gave them instructions to follow. Today and next week, we will see how well they followed those instructions.

Session starter (10 minutes)

- small piece of red yarn or cord

Option 1: Who has the scarlet cord?
Instruct kids to form a circle. Kids should stand, cup their hands behind their backs, and close their eyes. Explain that you will walk around the circle and place the scarlet cord in

Tip: Remind kids to keep their hands behind them the entire time. Otherwise, they will reveal who does not have the cord.

one kid's hands. Pause behind each player. After you have given someone the cord, finish moving around the circle, and then announce that everyone may open their eyes and take turns guessing who has the cord. Play several times.

Say • You had to guess who had the cord. The word *who* is part of today's big picture question. The Israelites had crossed the Jordan River. Now they must conquer the land. The first challenge they faced was a city with a big wall. To find out *who* has an important part in today's big picture question, we need to head to our large group. Listen closely to also find out what part a scarlet cord has in our Bible story.

Option 2: Quiet ball

Form two teams. Each team must spread out across the room in a zigzag formation. On your command, the first player in the line will toss the ball to the second player in the line. Each player will toss the ball until it reaches the end of the line. Challenge kids to pass the ball across the room seven times without speaking or making noise.

• foam balls or soft beanbags, 1 per team

Tip: If you do not have enough kids to form teams, allow kids to play with a partner and toss the ball back and forth seven times without speaking.

If a player drops a ball, he may pick it up and play from that point as long as no one on the team talks. If a player talks, the team must start over. When a team is completely finished, they must shout together "God is great!"

Say • God instructed the Israelites to follow His commands to defeat the city of Jericho. One of His commands involved being completely silent. Did the Israelites always obey God and His commands? Name one time they did not. We will learn how well the Israelites obeyed God's directions for defeating the city of Jericho in our Bible story.

Transition to large group

Large Group LEADER

Session Title: The Conquest of Jericho
Bible Passage: Joshua 2; 6
Big Picture Question: Who fought the battle of Jericho? God fought for His people and handed Jericho over to the Israelites.
Key Passage: Joshua 24:15
Unit Christ Connection: Joshua was a representation of Christ, leading the Israelites to victory in overcoming Canaan as Jesus leads us to victory in overcoming the world.

Countdown

• countdown video

Show the countdown video as your kids arrive, and set it to end as large group time begins.

Introduce the session (1 minute)

• pile of stones

[Large Group Leader enters and kneels next to a pile of stones as he begins to speak.]

Leader • This fort was built many, many years ago. It is so old that all we have are a few walls and some piles of stone from the old walls. If we had time to dig down into the ground, we might discover more stones. Imagine how strong and mighty this fort was back when it was built. Do you think the people who lived inside felt safe? Our Bible story today is about a big city with a big, strong wall all the way around it. The wall was designed to keep the people inside safe. Join me in looking at our timeline map to see what the name of this city was.

Timeline map (1 minute)

• Timeline Map

Leader • The title of our Bible story is "The Conquest of Jericho." Have you heard the word *conquest* before? The word *conquest* is related to the word *conquer*. To *conquer* is to overcome a people or place by force. God instructed the Israelites to conquer the promised land. Today we see the first conquest occurred at the city of Jericho.

Sing (5 minutes)

• "Our God" song

Leader • Before we look at the story of Jericho in the Book of Joshua, let's pause and remember what we have learned about God so far. Name something we have learned about God on our chronological journey through the Bible. Great answers! All of those answers are reasons that our God is one true God. He is mightier, stronger, and greater than anyone else!

Sing "Our God."

Big picture question (1 minute)

Leader • The Israelites faced a big battle in today's Bible story. Our big picture question is, *Who fought the battle of Jericho?* Wait a minute. Don't shout out an answer yet! You may think you know who fought the battle, but we need to examine our Bible story first. Open your Bibles to Joshua 2. Joshua comes after the Book of Deuteronomy, and it is close to the front of your Bible. Remember, anytime you need to find a book in the Bible you can turn to the front and find the table of contents or contents page. The table of contents page has a list of all the books of the Bible and the page numbers where you can find them.

• "The Conquest of Jericho" video
• Bibles
• Bible Story Picture Slide or Poster (enhanced CD)
• Big Picture Question Slide or Poster (enhanced CD)

Tell the Bible story (10 minutes)

Open your Bible to Joshua 2 and tell the Bible story in your own words, or show the Bible story video "The Conquest of Jericho."

Leader • Our big picture question is, *Who fought the battle of Jericho?* Shout out what you think the answer is. ***God fought for His people and handed Jericho over to the Israelites.*** God told Joshua exactly what to do to conquer Jericho. God fought for His people. He caused all the walls of Jericho to collapse so the Israelites were able to walk into Jericho and conquer the city. God ordered the Israelites to destroy the city. Only a few types of items like silver and gold were to be saved. Those items were for the treasury of the Lord. All other items were to be completely destroyed. The Israelites were not to keep anything from Jericho for themselves.

Because she followed God and protected the spies, Rahab and her family were saved. Later Rahab married one of the Israelite men. Her choice to follow God changed Rahab's life. Rahab is mentioned in Jesus' genealogy found in Matthew 1. The genealogy is the list of people in Jesus' family. Because Rahab chose to follow Jesus, the legacy of her family changed. Rahab became a member of Jesus' earthly family.

Why do you think God didn't want the Israelites to take anything from Jericho? Do you remember our Christ connection? God promised to provide for the Israelites. He would give them everything they needed. The Israelites needed to trust God and obey His commands.

God also promises to provide for His people today. Matthew 6:33 tells Christians to focus on God and His righteousness. To be *righteous* is to do what is right. God is perfectly righteous. He always does what is right. His ways and plans are always right. When we follow God, He will provide for us like He did for the Israelites.

The Gospel: God's Plan for me (optional)

- Bibles

Leader • God also provided for our greatest need. Our greatest need is to be rescued or saved from our sin. God sent Jesus to rescue us by paying the penalty for our sin. Use the guide provided to share with boys and girls how to become a Christian. Tell kids how they can respond, and provide counselors to speak with each kid individually. Encourage counselors to use open-ended questions to allow kids to determine the direction of the conversation.

- Key Passage Slide or Poster (enhanced CD)
- "Choose for Yourself" song

Key passage (5 minutes)

Leader • Who remembers where our key passage is found in the Bible? Yes. It is Joshua 24:15. Do I have a volunteer who would like to lead the group to read our key passage?

Select a volunteer to lead the group to read the key passage in unison.

Leader • Every day we have a choice to follow God's commands or to sin by following someone or something else. Following God is not always easy, but His ways and commands are perfect.

Sing "Choose for Yourself."

- "Unit 8 Session 2" discussion starter video

Discussion starter video (5 minutes)

Leader • God cared for the Israelites and fought the battle of Jericho. Have you ever been in a situation where you had to choose whether or not to help someone else? Check out this video and we'll talk about it.

Show the "Unit 8 Session 2" discussion starter video.

Leader • If God provides for us, should we help others? What could you do if you were watching someone being picked on? Should you do something?

Help kids verbalize an appropriate response based upon today's big picture question and Christ connection. If needed, prompt the conversation or restate the question.

Prayer (2 minutes)

[Kneel again beside the pile of stones from the fort.]

Leader •I don't think I will ever look at our old fort with its piles of old stone and not think about the city of Jericho. The walls of our fort have slowly worn away over time, but the walls of Jericho completely collapsed because God fought for His people.

Say our big picture question and answer with me. ***Who fought the battle of Jericho? God fought for His people and handed Jericho over to the Israelites.*** Next week we will continue the story of the Israelites and what happened at the city of Jericho.

Close in prayer, asking God to help kids trust that He will provide for their needs every day.

Dismiss to small groups

The Gospel: God's Plan for Me

Ask kids if they have ever heard the word *gospel*. Clarify that the word *gospel* means "good news." It is the message about Christ, the kingdom of God, and salvation. Use the following guide to share the gospel with kids.

God rules. Explain to kids that the Bible tells us God created everything, and He is in charge of everything. Invite a volunteer to read Genesis 1:1 from the Bible. Read Revelation 4:11 or Colossians 1:16-17 aloud and explain what these verses mean.

We sinned. Tell kids that since the time of Adam and Eve, everyone has chosen to disobey God. (Romans 3:23) The Bible calls this sin. Because God is holy, God cannot be around sin. Sin separates us from God and deserves God's punishment of death. (Romans 6:23)

God provided. Choose a child to read John 3:16 aloud. Say that God sent His Son, Jesus, the perfect solution to our sin problem, to rescue us from the punishment we deserve. It's something we, as sinners, could never earn on our own. Jesus alone saves us. Read and explain Ephesians 2:8-9.

Jesus gives. Share with kids that Jesus lived a perfect life, died on the cross for our sins, and rose again. Because Jesus gave up His life for us, we can be welcomed into God's family for eternity. This is the best gift ever! Read Romans 5:8; 2 Corinthians 5:21; or 1 Peter 3:18.

We respond. Tell kids that they can respond to Jesus. Read Romans 10:9-10,13. Review these aspects of our response: Believe in your heart that Jesus alone saves you through what He's already done on the cross. Repent, turning from self and sin to Jesus. Tell God and others that your faith is in Jesus.

Offer to talk with any child who is interested in responding to Jesus.

Small Group LEADER

Session Title: The Conquest of Jericho
Bible Passage: Joshua 2; 6
Big Picture Question: Who fought the battle of Jericho? God fought for His people and handed Jericho over to the Israelites.
Key Passage: Joshua 24:15
Unit Christ Connection: Joshua was a representation of Christ, leading the Israelites to victory in overcoming Canaan as Jesus leads us to victory in overcoming the world.

- Bibles, 1 per kid
- Small Group Visual Pack
- chart paper
- markers or crayons

Option: Guide kids to create the individual pieces and tape them to the large piece of chart paper to form the newspaper.

Bible story review & Bible skills (10 minutes)

Guide kids to create a newspaper front page about today's Bible story. Kids need to create a headline and an article. Allow kids to be creative by drawing pictures. If you have a large group, form smaller groups of kids and lead each group to create its own newspaper. Encourage kids to look at Joshua 2 and Joshua 6 to find quotes for the article.

Say • *Who fought the battle of Jericho? God fought for His people and handed Jericho over to the Israelites.*

- Who meets our greatest need? (*Jesus meets our greatest need—to be saved from our sin. We can trust Him for our salvation.*)
- Jesus told His followers in Matthew 6 that following God's commands and seeking His righteousness is what they should focus on. God will provide for His people's needs when they follow Him.

If you choose to review with boys and girls how to become a Christian, explain that kids are welcome to speak with you or another teacher if they have questions.

- **God rules.** God created and is in charge of everything. (Gen. 1:1; Rev. 4:11; Col. 1:16-17)

- **We sinned.** Since Adam and Eve, everyone has chosen to disobey God. (Rom. 3:23; 6:23)
- **God provided.** God sent His Son Jesus to rescue us from the punishment we deserve. (John 3:16; Eph. 2:8-9)
- **Jesus gives.** Jesus lived a perfect life, died on the cross for our sins, and rose again so we can be welcomed into God's family. (Rom. 5:8; 2 Cor. 5:21; 1 Pet. 3:18)
- **We respond.** Believe that Jesus alone saves you. Repent. Tell God that your faith is in Jesus. (Rom. 10:9-10,13)

Review the timeline in the small group visual pack.

Key passage activity (5 minutes)

- Key Passage Poster (enhanced CD)
- sticky notes or small pieces of paper
- tape

Option: Write the key passage on a dry erase board and erase the words.

- "Jericho Gameboard" (enhanced CD)
- game markers such as buttons or small pieces of paper
- numbered cube
- Small Group Visual Pack

Lead kids to say the key passage quietly. Cover every seventh word and say the key passage again. Repeat covering every seventh word. Kids must say the key passage in a quiet voice until all the words are covered. On the final recitation, allow kids to shout the key passage.

Say • Following God's instructions was an important part of the Israelites' covenant with God. God defeated Jericho for the Israelites. All the Israelites had to do was obey God's instructions for the battle, including being quiet as they marched until the very end.

Activity choice (10 minutes)

Option 1: Jericho board game

Review Matthew 6:33. Provide each boy and girl with a gameboard marker. Allow the youngest kid in the group to start the game. To play, he will have 30 seconds to share one way he can follow God's commands and seek His righteousness. Review the definition of *righteous* (doing what is right). If he names something within the 30 seconds, he may roll a numbered cube to determine how many spaces he may move on the gameboard. Instruct players to take turns until someone reaches the end of the gameboard.

If time remains, play again, but ask kids to name a way someone in the Bible followed God's commands and sought His righteousness. Use the timeline in the small group visual pack to help kids recall previous Bible stories.

Say • *Who fought the battle of Jericho? God fought for His people and handed Jericho over to the Israelites.*

   • God provided for the needs of His people.
   • What is a need we have that God provides for us?
   • Who meets our greatest need? (*Jesus meets our greatest need—to be saved from our sin. We can trust Him for our salvation.*)

- graham crackers
- red candy lacing
- icing tubes
- paper plates
- paper towels
- wet wipes or damp paper towels
- ziplock bags (optional)

Tip: If you have kids who are allergic to wet wipes, provide the entire class with damp paper towels.

Tip: Kids may ask about the word *prostitute*. Be prepared to provide a short, age-appropriate response if needed.

Option 2: Rahab's wall snack

Instruct kids to place a graham cracker on a paper towel or plate to form a section of Jericho's wall. Use decorating icing tubes to draw windows on Jericho's wall. Position a piece of red candy lacing from one of the windows.

Remind kids of the command the spies gave Rahab about the scarlet cord (Josh. 2:17-21). Lead kids to find Matthew 1:5 and Hebrews 11:31 in the Bible and read about Rahab's legacy. Allow kids to create more panels of the wall. Either allow kids to eat the snack or provide ziplock bags to transport the snack home for eating later.

Say • Rahab was a member of Jesus' family. Rahab chose to leave behind her old life to follow God with the Israelites. After Jericho was defeated, one of the Israelites married Rahab and she became a part of the Israelite community. She was an important part of God's plan to send Jesus to be our Lord and Savior.

•Who fought the battle of Jericho? God fought for His people and handed Jericho over to the Israelites.

• pencils
• journals
• Bibles
• Journal Page, 1 per kid (enhanced CD)
• "Dot Message" activity page, 1 per kid

Option: Allow each kid to cut pictures from a magazine of items that God provided for his or her family.

Journal and prayer (5 minutes)

Guide each kid to spend a few minutes writing or drawing on the journal page about a time God provided for one of her needs.

Say *•Who fought the battle of Jericho? God fought for His people and handed Jericho over to the Israelites.*

• Who meets our greatest need? (*Jesus meets our greatest need—to be saved from our sin. We can trust Him for our salvation.*)

As times allows, lead kids to complete the activity page, "Dot Message," to reveal a reminder of who will help us in times of need.

Teacher BIBLE STUDY

When the Israelites conquered Jericho, God told them not to take anything. Everything in the city was to be destroyed and set apart for God. Achan must have assumed no one would notice if he kept a few things for himself. The cloak was beautiful, and he sure could use some pieces of silver and a bar of gold. No harm, no foul. Right?

Wrong. God had commanded complete obedience from the Israelites. God knew what Achan had done, and His anger burned against all of the Israelites.

Joshua sent spies into the land of Ai. There were only a few people in Ai. Joshua sent a few thousand men to fight, but during the battle, the Israelites ran away in fear. About 36 of them were killed. Joshua knew something was wrong. He suspected God had lied to the Israelites about protecting them against their enemies. He cried out to God, "Why did you bring us across the Jordan to die at the hand of the Amorites?" (Josh. 7:7).

Joshua had it all wrong. God explained that the Israelites had sinned against Him—that was why they had not won the battle.

The next morning, God revealed that it was Achan who had sinned. Joshua brought Achan forward to confess his sin. Achan's possessions were destroyed, and Achan and his family were stoned to death. The Israelites covered their bodies with a large pile of stones as a reminder of the consequences of sin.

God hates sin. (See Prov. 6:16-19.) God deals with sin by punishing it. We are all sinners. Here's the bad news: "For the wages of sin is death," but here's the good news: "but the gift of God is eternal life in Christ Jesus our Lord" (Rom. 6:23). We all deserve to die for our sin, but Jesus came to bear the consequences for us by dying on the cross in our place.

Older Kids BIBLE STUDY OVERVIEW

Session Title: Achan Sinned
Bible Passage: Joshua 7
Big Picture Question: How does God feel about sin? God hates sin and punishes sin.
Key Passage: Joshua 24:15
Unit Christ Connection: Joshua was a representation of Christ, leading the Israelites to victory in overcoming Canaan as Jesus leads us to victory in overcoming the world.

Small Group Opening

Large Group Leader

Small Group Leader

The BIBLE STORY

Achan Sinned
Joshua 7

When the people of Israel attacked Jericho, God gave them one rule: Destroy everything. Keep nothing for yourselves. But one man, Achan (AY kuhn), disobeyed God. God was angry with the Israelites because of Achan's disobedience.

Joshua sent men from Jericho to a city called Ai (AY igh) to spy out the land. The men went and spied out Ai. They came back and said, "Do not send all of the men to attack Ai. There are not very many people there; you only need to send two or three thousand." So about 3,000 men went to Ai. They ran away from the men of Ai, and about 36 of them were killed. The men were very afraid.

Joshua tore his clothes and fell to the ground before the ark of the LORD. The elders did the same thing, and they all put dust on their heads. Joshua asked God, "Why did you bring us across the Jordan River just to have us killed by these people? We should have been content to stay out of the promised land! When the other people living in this land hear that we ran scared from the men of Ai, they will surround us and attack us!"

The LORD said to Joshua, "Stand up! Israel has sinned and disobeyed My covenant. They have taken some of the things I told them not to. This is why they cannot defeat their enemies. I will no longer be with you until you remove from you the things I told you to destroy."

God continued, "Go and tell the people to make themselves clean. In the morning, they should present themselves by tribe. When I pick out a tribe, that tribe should present itself clan by clan. I will select one clan; that clan is to come forward family by family. I will select one family, and that family should come forward man by man. You should punish the man who is caught with the forbidden things. Destroy him and everything he has because he has disobeyed God."

Joshua got up early the next morning. Israel came forward tribe by tribe, clan by clan, family by family, and man by man. Achan was chosen from all the people. He was the one who had taken the forbidden things.

"Confess to the LORD. Tell me what you have done," Joshua said to

Achan. "Don't hide anything from me."

Achan replied, "It's true. I have sinned against God. When we overtook Jericho, I saw a beautiful cloak, some pieces of silver, and a bar of gold. I wanted them very badly, so I took them. They are buried in the ground in my tent."

Joshua sent messengers to Achan's tent to collect the things. They laid them before Joshua. "Why have you caused trouble for us?" Joshua asked. "Today God will trouble you!" The people of Israel killed Achan and his family. They covered their bodies with a big pile of rocks. God was no longer angry with Israel.

Christ Connection: The punishment for Achan's sin was death. It seems harsh, but the Bible says that the wages of sin is death. (Romans 6:23) Because we sin, we deserve to die too. Jesus came to die in our place. When we confess our sins and trust in Jesus, we are forgiven and saved from spiritual death.

Small Group OPENING

Session Title: Achan Sinned
Bible Passage: Joshua 7
Big Picture Question: How does God feel about sin? God hates sin and punishes sin.
Key Passage: Joshua 24:15
Unit Christ Connection: Joshua was a representation of Christ, leading the Israelites to victory in overcoming Canaan as Jesus leads us to victory in overcoming the world.

Tip: Be sensitive to kids' responses. Kids may misread your response or shut down if they do not believe you are respectful of the responses they provide.

- "Bible Banners" activity page, 1 per kid
- pencils
- Bibles, 1 per kid

Welcome time

Greet kids. Use this time to collect the offering, fill out attendance sheets, and help new kids connect to your group. Ask kids to share their favorite feeling or emotion and what they think is the worst feeling or emotion.

Activity page (5 minutes)

Guide kids to use the Bible to locate the Scriptures and complete the activity page, "Bible Banners."

Say • Sin has serious consequences. It separates us from God. In our previous Bible stories, did the Israelites have a problem with sin? Thankfully, God provided the way for us to be rescued from our sin—Jesus.

Session starter (10 minutes)

Option 1: One, two, three, how do you feel?
Form pairs. Pairs must face each other but look down. Instruct kids that you will read a statement and say the phrase "One, two, three, how do you feel?" At that point kids must look up and show the emotion they would have if the situation happened to them. Each kid may have a sad face, happy face, mad face, or confused face. Challenge

partners to count how many times they have the same faces.

Sample scenarios: Your dog ran away. Your birthday present was broken when you opened it. You received exactly what you wanted for Christmas. A friend told a lie about you. You tried out for the team but didn't make it. Your parents planned a trip to an amusement park for vacation. Your grandparents sent you a dollar in the mail. You made an A on your math test.

Say • What are some other emotions you feel at times? How do you feel when you sin? How do other people feel when you sin? How do you think God feels when His people sin? In our Bible story today we will learn more about the consequences of sin.

• paper
• pens or pencils

Option 2: Seeking signatures

Lead each kid to collect a signature from one friend for each of the categories you name. Kids should seek to gain as many different signatures as possible.

• a friend with brown eyes
• a friend with a pet
• a friend with a video gaming system
• a friend with shoelaces on his or her shoes today
• a friend whose favorite color is blue or purple
• a friend who has a brother or sister
• a friend who does not have any siblings
• a friend who likes to play soccer
• a friend who loves cheese pizza
• a friend who is wearing red

Say • You were seeking to find friends in today's game. In our Bible story, Joshua had to seek to find a person who hid some items in the Israelite camp.

Transition to large group

Joshua

Large Group LEADER

Session Title: Achan Sinned
Bible Passage: Joshua 7
Big Picture Question: How does God feel about sin? God hates sin and punishes sin.
Key Passage: Joshua 24:15
Unit Christ Connection: Joshua was a representation of Christ, leading the Israelites to victory in overcoming Canaan as Jesus leads us to victory in overcoming the world.

Countdown

• countdown video

Show the countdown video as your kids arrive, and set it to end as large group time begins.

Introduce the session (2 minutes)

[Large Group Leader enters looking sad.]

Leader • Hey, everyone. How are you? I'm sad. My brother did something that really hurt me. My brother stole my favorite, best, most amazing, awesome, totally cool coin given to me by my grandfather. It was a special present for my birthday last year. I wanted to bring it to show you, but I couldn't find it anywhere. It was missing. I searched. I hunted. I looked everywhere. Finally, my brother confessed that he had taken it and lost it. It really hurt my feelings that he would take something from me. Do you have something special you would be sad to lose?

Have any of you ever been hurt because someone else sinned? You have. Was it hard to forgive that person? Yes, I know what you mean. It was really hard to forgive my brother, but I did. Still, I'm just a little sad that it happened. Did you know that your sin could hurt someone else? Yes. The Israelites learned that lesson and some others in today's Bible story.

Before we look at our timeline map, we need to stand up and march a little. We didn't practice our marching last week, so let's practice today. Everyone stand up and follow me. Left, left, left, right, left. Left, left, left, right, left. Good marching! Everyone can have a seat again.

Timeline map (1 minute)

• Timeline Map

Point to each story on the map and timeline as you review.

Leader •Our time here at this old fort has been a lot of fun. Who remembers one of the Bible stories we have heard the last two weeks? Good. God stopped the water in the Jordan River so the Israelites could cross. They built a memorial of 12 stones to remember how God had saved and sustained them.

Next, the Israelites conquered the city of Jericho. What did God tell the Israelites to do after the walls fell down? Right! God instructed the Israelites to put some things in the treasury of the LORD and to destroy everything else. Today we are going to hear what happened to the Israelites after the battle of Jericho.

Big picture question (1 minute)

Leader •Our big picture question is, *How does God feel about sin?* I need one volunteer to tell me what you think. Call on one kid to provide an answer.

Leader •That is a good answer. We are going to look at our Bible story to find the answer to our big picture question.

• "Achan Sinned" video
• Bibles
• Bible Story Picture Slide or Poster (enhanced CD)
• Big Picture Question Slide or Poster (enhanced CD)

Tell the Bible story (9 minutes)

Open your Bible to Joshua 7 and tell the Bible story in your own words, or show the Bible story video "Achan Sinned."

Leader •Achan's sin had serious consequences. He died because of his sin. Sin is breaking God's laws. Our big picture question is, *How does God feel about sin?* The answer is, *God hates sin and punishes sin.* Because God is holy, He cannot be around sin. Because He is just, He cannot allow sin to occur without consequences. Sin has a price. The price is that sin separates us from God. God wants His people to obey Him. He wants them to be holy because He is holy.

Sin can also affect other people. The Israelites suffered because of Achan's sin. They went into battle, but God did not fight for them because of Achan's sin. Men died because of Achan's sin. Sin is always serious and always has consequences.

Did you notice that Achan thought he could hide his sin? He thought no one would know about the items he took because he hid them. Do we ever try to hide our sin? Sometimes, but God always knows about our sin. When we sin, we should confess it to God and seek His forgiveness. Trying to hide that we've sinned never helps.

The Gospel: God's Plan for Me (optional)

• Bible

Leader •The Bible tells us that the price of sin is spiritual death, an eternal separation from God. Thankfully, Jesus paid the price for our sin. We can confess our sin and trust Jesus. We can be forgiven and saved from spiritual death or separation from God.

Use the guide provided to share with boys and girls how to become a Christian. Allow kids an opportunity to respond by having counselors available to speak with each kid individually.

Discussion starter video (5 minutes)

Leader • *How does God feel about sin? God hates sin and punishes sin.* Achan's sin affected other people. Watch this video and we'll talk about it.

Show the "Unit 8 Session 3" discussion starter video.

Leader • What was happening at the end of the video? Was it a mess? Chaotic? What caused all the mess? Yes, one little action created all the mess. That's called a chain reaction. What chain reaction did Achan's sin cause? Can our sin cause a chain reaction and affect other people?

Help kids understand that sin can impact more than just the person who sinned.

Key passage (5 minutes)

Leader • Our key passage is a reminder of the covenant God made with the Israelites. They could choose to follow God and receive all the promises and blessings He promised, or they could refuse to follow God and receive none of His blessings. Do I have a volunteer who would like to say the key passage for the group?

Select one or two volunteers to share the key passage from memory. Lead the remaining kids to read the key passage and to sing "Choose for Yourself."

Sing (5 minutes)

Leader • Our God is worthy of our praise. We can trust Him to help us, provide for us, and guide us. Join me in singing our theme song. Remember that God will be with us. We can choose to follow Him and obey His commands.

Sing "Our God." Ask a couple of kids to share their favorite line of the song and what it tells them about God.

Prayer (2 minutes)

Leader • *How does God feel about sin? God hates sin and punishes sin.* The story of Achan is a sad story. Achan knew God's commands about the city of Jericho, but he chose to sin. Sin always has consequences. We can learn from the story of Achan. It is a reminder to us that our sin not only affect us, but it can affect other people too.

God is serious about sin, and He is serious about forgiveness. If we ask Him for forgiveness, He will freely give it to us. We may still have consequences for our sin, but we are forgiven. God is so serious about forgiveness that He sent His Son, Jesus, to die on the cross in our place. We can be forgiven when we confess our sin and trust Jesus as our Savior and Lord.

If you have any questions about becoming a Christian or being forgiven for your sin, please come talk to me or another one of the teachers in our room.

After I pray, watch your small group leader for the signal for you to march to your small group.

Close in prayer.

Dismiss to small groups

The Gospel: God's Plan for Me

Ask kids if they have ever heard the word *gospel*. Clarify that the word *gospel* means "good news." It is the message about Christ, the kingdom of God, and salvation. Use the following guide to share the gospel with kids.

God rules. Explain to kids that the Bible tells us God created everything, and He is in charge of everything. Invite a volunteer to read Genesis 1:1 from the Bible. Read Revelation 4:11 or Colossians 1:16-17 aloud and explain what these verses mean.

We sinned. Tell kids that since the time of Adam and Eve, everyone has chosen to disobey God. (Romans 3:23) The Bible calls this sin. Because God is holy, God cannot be around sin. Sin separates us from God and deserves God's punishment of death. (Romans 6:23)

God provided. Choose a child to read John 3:16 aloud. Say that God sent His Son, Jesus, the perfect solution to our sin problem, to rescue us from the punishment we deserve. It's something we, as sinners, could never earn on our own. Jesus alone saves us. Read and explain Ephesians 2:8-9.

Jesus gives. Share with kids that Jesus lived a perfect life, died on the cross for our sins, and rose again. Because Jesus gave up His life for us, we can be welcomed into God's family for eternity. This is the best gift ever! Read Romans 5:8; 2 Corinthians 5:21; or 1 Peter 3:18.

We respond. Tell kids that they can respond to Jesus. Read Romans 10:9-10,13. Review these aspects of our response: Believe in your heart that Jesus alone saves you through what He's already done on the cross. Repent, turning from self and sin to Jesus. Tell God and others that your faith is in Jesus.

Offer to talk with any child who is interested in responding to Jesus.

Small Group LEADER

Session Title: Achan Sinned
Bible Passage: Joshua 7
Big Picture Question: How does God feel about sin? God hates sin and
punishes sin.
Key Passage: Joshua 24:15
Unit Christ Connection: Joshua was a representation of Christ, leading
the Israelites to victory in overcoming Canaan as Jesus leads us to
victory in overcoming the world.

- Bibles, 1 per kid
- Small Group Visual Pack
- index cards
- marker or pen

Bible story review & Bible skills (10 minutes)

Review the timeline in the small group visual pack. Help
kids connect Achan to the story of Jericho.

Prior to small group, write the answers to the following
review questions on index cards. Place the cards where all
the kids can see them or distribute cards to kids. When you
ask a review question, allow kids to find the answer in the
Scripture passage and identify which index card has the
right answer.

1. Which of God's commands did an Israelite break
   when the people destroyed Jericho? (*Do not take
   anything for yourself; Josh. 6:17-19; 7:11*)
2. Which city did Israel try unsuccessfully to defeat?
   (*Ai; Josh. 7:2,5*)
3. Why did Israel lose the battle of Ai? (*An Israelite
   had disobeyed God, Josh. 7:11-12*)
4. Who disobeyed God? (*Achan, Josh. 7:18-20*)
5. What did Achan take? (*a cloak, pieces of silver, a
   bar of gold; Josh. 7:21*)
6. Where did Achan put the things he took? (*He
   buried them in the ground inside his tent,
   Josh. 7:21*)

Bonus questions:

7. ***How does God feel about sin? God hates sin and punishes sin.***

8. Who came to die in our place? (*Jesus came to die in our place. When we confess our sins and trust in Jesus, we are forgiven and saved from spiritual death.*)

If you choose to review with boys and girls how to become a Christian, explain that kids are always welcome to speak with you or another teacher if they have questions.

- **God rules.** God created and is in charge of everything. (Gen. 1:1; Rev. 4:11; Col. 1:16-17)
- **We sinned.** Since Adam and Eve, everyone has chosen to disobey God. (Rom. 3:23; 6:23)
- **God provided.** God sent His Son Jesus to rescue us from the punishment we deserve. (John 3:16; Eph. 2:8-9)
- **Jesus gives.** Jesus lived a perfect life, died on the cross for our sins, and rose again so we can be welcomed into God's family. (Rom. 5:8; 2 Cor. 5:21; 1 Pet. 3:18)
- **We respond.** Believe that Jesus alone saves you. Repent. Tell God that your faith is in Jesus. (Rom. 10:9-10,13)

Key passage activity (5 minutes)

- Key Passage Poster (enhanced CD)
- tape
- index cards
- markers

Print the key passage on index cards. Tape an index card to each kid. Instruct kids to line up in the correct order and read the key passage together. For an added twist, give kids more than one card so they must keep moving to get the correct order.

Say • Try to memorize the first half of the key passage this week if you haven't memorized it yet.

Activity choice (10 minutes)

Option 1: Obey actions

Guide kids to form two or three teams. Each team must think of an action to perform silently for the other teams to try to guess. The action must be a rule to obey or something a kid does to obey. (Examples: vacuuming, dusting, putting away toys, ironing clothes, no running inside, no talking while someone else is talking)

Say • *How does God feel about sin? God hates sin and punishes sin.*

   • Do you ever have trouble following any of the rules you demonstrated? Has anyone broken one of these rules? Sometimes it is easier to sin than to follow God, or at least we think that. But God always promises to help His people. When we are tempted to disobey, we can ask God for help.

   • What do you think could have happened if Achan had stopped and asked God to help him resist the temptation? Maybe that would have happened. We don't know. But we do know that God will forgive us when we ask Him to forgive us for our sin. And He will help us resist sin if we ask.

Option 2: Sin wall art

• scrap paper
• pens
• tape or other method of attaching paper to the wall
• bowl

Option: Place the papers on the floor.

Guide boys and girls to write on pieces of scrap paper sins people commit. Notify kids that you will read each one aloud. Lead kids to wad up each sin into a ball and toss them into the bowl. Open and read each paper one at a time.

Discuss each sin and why the kids think people commit that sin. Tape the pieces of paper on the wall backward (no print showing) in the form of the word *sin* or *death*. Lead kids to open their Bibles and read Romans 6:23. Explain to kids that sin leads to spiritual death or separation from God.

Say • Sin separates us from God. It leads to a spiritual death or separation. Sin keeps us from knowing and loving God. Sin has serious consequences. We have hope because Jesus came and died for our sin. We can be forgiven of our sin. In today's Bible story we heard the horrible price of sin. God doesn't want His people to sin. God wants His people to be holy because He is holy.

• Who came to die in our place? (*Jesus came to die in our place. When we confess our sins and trust in Jesus, we are forgiven and saved from spiritual death.*)

Review how to become a Christian and allow kids to ask any questions. Ask kids to share how they would tell a friend about how to become a Christian. What would they say first? Call on multiple kids to respond.

Journal and prayer (5 minutes)

• pencils
• journals
• Bibles, 1 per kid
• Journal Page, 1 per kid (enhanced CD)
• "Gospel Connection" activity page, 1 per kid

Allow each kid to write a prayer to God. Kids may write a prayer of confession. They may write a prayer asking God to help them resist sin. They may wish to write a prayer telling God something else. Also encourage kids to write down any prayer requests they may have.

Say • Who came to die in our place? (*Jesus came to die in our place. When we confess our sins and trust in Jesus, we are forgiven and saved from spiritual death.*)

Close in prayer.

As time allows, review the gospel as kids complete the activity page, "Gospel Connection." Help kids use the Bible to check their answers.

Teacher BIBLE STUDY

The Israelites' battle with the men of Ai (AY igh) was fresh in their minds. Achan sinned after the conquering of Jericho, and God was not with the Israelites in battle against Ai. They had run away, scared. Thirty-six of them died. Joshua and the Israelites stoned Achan and his family and buried them beneath a large pile of stones as God commanded. These memorial stones reminded the people what we read in Romans 6:23: "The wages of sin is death."

God gave the Israelites another chance. God helped them destroy Jericho; now He would help them destroy Ai—except this time God allowed them to plunder the city, keeping goods and livestock for themselves. God was going to give them victory!

Joshua sent a group of men to hide in wait behind the city. The rest of the men approached Ai. The king of Ai saw them coming and sent all of his men out to fight them. Israel retreated into the wilderness, and the men of Ai followed. The city was completely unprotected. Joshua raised his sword toward Ai, and the men in hiding ambushed the city. Joshua and his men turned and defeated the men of Ai. Then Joshua burned the city to the ground.

After their victory, Joshua built an altar to the LORD. They offered burnt offerings and sacrificed peace offerings. Joshua read the book of the law to the people.

God's presence with Israel was tied directly to their obedience to Him. Because of our faith in Jesus Christ, God is always with us, and we are victorious over our enemies of sin and death. Because of our faith and trust in Jesus, we have right standing with God.

Older Kids BIBLE STUDY OVERVIEW

Session Title: The Defeat of Ai
Bible Passage: Joshua 8
Big Picture Question: What does God do when we obey Him? God blesses people who obey Him in faith.
Key Passage: Joshua 24:15
Unit Christ Connection: Joshua was a representation of Christ, leading the Israelites to victory in overcoming Canaan as Jesus leads us to victory in overcoming the world.

Small Group Opening

Large Group Leader

Small Group Leader

The BIBLE STORY

The Defeat of Ai
Joshua 8

God said to Joshua, "Do not be afraid or discouraged. Take all of your men with you and go up to attack Ai. I will give you victory over the king of Ai, all of the people, the city, and its land. You may keep all of the livestock and possessions for yourselves."

God told Joshua to set up an ambush behind the city. So Joshua selected 30,000 men. He sent them out at night to lie in wait behind the city. Joshua told them to be ready to attack Ai.

Joshua had a plan: The rest of the army would go with him toward the city. "When they come out against us," Joshua said, "we will run away like we did before. We will lead them away from the city, then the ambush will take over the city. Then we will set the city on fire!" It was the perfect plan.

Joshua told the people to obey God's commands for attacking the city. Early the next morning, Joshua and his men went out toward the city. The king of Ai saw them and sent his men out to fight them. When the enemy army got near, Joshua and the Israelites ran away. They pretended to be afraid. The army of Ai followed them. Both armies moved away from the city of Ai. The people of Ai had no idea that Joshua had thousands of men hiding on the other side of the city. The army of Ai left the city completely unprotected.

God said to Joshua, "Hold your sword in your hand toward Ai, for I will hand the city over to you." So Joshua held out his sword. The men hiding in wait overtook the city. They set the city on fire.

The men of Ai saw that the city was burning. The Israelites stopped running away and turned to fight the army of Ai. Israel's enemies realized they were trapped! The Israelites had moved in on both sides of them. The men of Ai had no way to escape. All the people of Ai were struck down. The Israelites took for themselves the livestock and all the goods in the city, as God had told them to do.

At that time Joshua built an altar to the Lord, just as Moses had commanded the Israelites. He built it according to what was written in the book of the law, which Moses wrote down. The Israelites sacrificed offerings to God. Joshua read aloud the words of the law. Everyone heard all of the laws that Moses had commanded—from the women to the little children to the foreigners who were with them.

Christ Connection: The Israelites were under a covenant in which their obedience was directly related to God's presence with them. We are under a new covenant through Jesus Christ, who took the punishment for our sin on Himself. Because of Christ, we are in right standing with God. We are victorious over our enemies because of our faith in Christ. (Romans 8:37)

Small Group OPENING

Session Title: The Defeat of Ai
Bible Passage: Joshua 8
Big Picture Question: What does God do when we obey Him? God blesses people who obey Him in faith.
Key Passage: Joshua 24:15
Unit Christ Connection: Joshua was a representation of Christ, leading the Israelites to victory in overcoming Canaan as Jesus leads us to victory in overcoming the world.

Welcome time

Greet each kid as he or she arrives. Use this time to collect the offering, fill out attendance sheets, and help new kids connect to your group. Ask kids to share a time it was difficult for them to obey God or their parents. Encourage kids that obeying in faith can be hard, but it always honors God.

Activity page (5 minutes)

- "Obey Puzzles" activity page, 1 per kid
- pencils
- Bible

Guide kids to complete the activity page, "Obey Puzzles." If a kid doesn't know how to look up a verse in the Bible, show all the kids how to find a book by using the table of contents page at the front of the Bible.

Say • Does anyone have a guess about what our Bible story may be about today? Your activity page is a clue. Yes. Our Bible story is about obeying in faith.

Session starter (10 minutes)

Option 1: Back tag

Say • Has anyone heard of an ambush before? What is it? An *ambush* is a type of attack where people wait to surprise the people they are attacking.

Older Kids Bible Study Leader Guide
Unit 8 • Session 4
© 2012 LifeWay Christian Resources

Lead kids to play a game of tag. Explain that kids may only tag someone on the back. If your teaching space is not adequate for running, lead kids to play on their knees and restrict the area kids can move within. If too many kids are easily tagged, allow only one kid to tag the other kids. Or designate one kid to *unfreeze* kids who have been tagged.

Say •I asked you about an ambush before we played our game because an ambush is exactly what happened in our Bible story. In today's Bible story, people were surprised by an ambush that came from behind them. Was anyone tagged on the back and it surprised you—you didn't see the person until you felt the tag? Listen to discover whether the Israelites ambushed someone or if someone else ambushed the Israelites.

Option 2: O-B-E-Y spell it!

• large containers of foam letters, 2

Form two teams. Provide each team with a container of foam letters. Challenge each team to find the letters to spell the word *obey* as many times as possible in three minutes.

Say •What happens when we obey God in faith? What is God's response? We will learn more about God's response to our obedience of faith in large group.

Transition to large group

Large Group LEADER

Session Title: The Defeat of Ai
Bible Passage: Joshua 8
Big Picture Question: What does God do when we obey Him? God blesses people who obey Him in faith.
Key Passage: Joshua 24:15
Unit Christ Connection: Joshua was a representation of Christ, leading the Israelites to victory in overcoming Canaan as Jesus leads us to victory in overcoming the world.

• countdown video

Countdown

Show the countdown video as your kids arrive, and set it to end as large group time begins.

Introduce the session (1 minute)

• map

Tip: Any map will do. Consider marking the map with stick figures to show an ambush.

[Large Group Leader enters the room, intently studying a map. Take several steps before noticing the kids.]

Leader • Hello, friends! I'm glad to see you are back at our old fort site. I found this really cool map here at the fort. It shows the plans for a battle. Over here you can see the city with a group of soldiers. Over here a group of soldiers is waiting in front of the city. And on this side, the map shows a group of soldiers hiding behind the city waiting for the battle. This map shows an ambush.

Did you know there is an ambush in today's Bible story? Yes, we do have an ambush. Before we turn to our Bible story, I need to tell you the big picture question.

Big picture question (1 minute)

Leader • *What does God do when we obey Him?* The Israelites have had quite a history of obeying God one time and disobeying God another time. In today's Bible story, the Israelites chose to obey in faith. We are going to find out what happens when God's people obey in faith.

What do you think the answer is to our big picture question? I think some of you may be right. Open your Bibles to Joshua 8, and we'll explore today's Bible story and discover more about the ambush that occurred.

Tell the Bible story (9 minutes)

- "The Defeat of Ai" Bible story video
- Bibles
- Bible Story Picture Slide or Poster (enhanced CD)
- Big Picture Question Slide or Poster (enhanced CD)

Open your Bible to Joshua 8 and tell the Bible story in your own words, or show the Bible story video "The Defeat of Ai."

Leader • In our last Bible story, the Israelites tried to conquer Ai, but they lost because Achan had sinned. The Israelites ran away in defeat. This time, God instructed Joshua to take his troops and attack Ai. God promised that He would give the Israelites the victory. Joshua's plan was to make Ai think the Israelites were running away again, but this time they weren't running away. They planned an ambush.

Do you remember our big picture question? *What does God do when we obey Him?* The Israelites learned that *God blesses people who obey Him in faith*. Read the big picture question and answer with me. *What does God do when we obey Him? God blesses people who obey Him in faith.* Now that the Israelites obeyed God in faith, God blessed them. The Israelites won. To bless someone is to provide someone with something good. God blesses His people with something good when they obey Him in faith.

Does God always bless obedience of faith to His will? Yes. Sometimes we don't immediately see how God blesses our obedience of faith. God's blessings aren't always visible. We usually aren't fighting battles to conquer cities like the Israelites were. But God does bless our obedience of faith. One of the ways God blesses our obedience of faith is that He is with us, helping us obey Him in faith. The way God blesses our obedience of faith isn't always the way we think He will bless us. Sometimes He will bless us in a way we don't really recognize right away. What are some good things God has blessed you with? Sometimes God blesses our obedience of faith in ways we don't expect.

The Bible tells Christians that because of Jesus, we can have a right relationship with God. We can know God, love God, and obey God in faith. We can be victorious over our enemies because of Jesus. That does not mean that everything will always happen the way we want it to. It doesn't mean that no one will ever be mean to us or hurt our feelings. What it means is that as Christians, we have Jesus on our side helping us endure hard times. Ultimately, Christians will be victorious over sin and spend eternity with Jesus.

The Gospel: God's Plan for Me (optional)

• Bible

Use Scripture and the guide provided to explain to boys and girls how to become a Christian. Give kids an opportunity to respond and speak with a counselor one-on-one.

Timeline map (2 minutes)

• Timeline Map

Leader • From the beginning, God planned to send Jesus to rescue us from sin. The Israelites were a part of God's plan to send Jesus. Let's review some of our previous stories by looking at our timeline map.

Review the previous Bible stories. Emphasize the Israelites' defeat at Ai in the previous week's story and today's victory at Ai to help kids see how God blesses obedience of faith.

Sing (5 minutes)

• "Our God" song

Leader •Now that we've remembered all the things our God has done, let's spend some time worshiping Him for all of those things.

Lead kids to sing "Our God."

Discussion starter video (5 minutes)

• "Unit 8 Session 4" discussion starter video

Leader •Remember last week when we talked about a chain reaction? Can you have a good chain reaction? Think about that question while you watch this video.

Watch the "Unit 8 Session 4" discussion starter video.

Leader •What do you think? Do good chain reactions happen? Our big picture question and answer was, ***What does God do when we obey Him? God blesses people who obey Him in faith.*** Do you think God could use you to bless someone else?

Key passage (5 minutes)

• Key Passage Slide or Poster (enhanced CD)
• "Choose for Yourself" song

Leader •We have two more weeks to memorize our key passage. Remember, we have a choice whether or not to follow God. Also remember our big picture question. ***What does God do when we obey Him? God blesses people who obey Him in faith.***

Read the key passage. Lead kids to say the passage. Invite the boys to say the first word, the girls to say the second word, the boys will say the third word, and so forth. Sing "Choose for Yourself."

Prayer (2 minutes)

Leader •*What does God do when we obey Him? God blesses people who obey Him in faith.* What are some possible ways God blesses obedience of faith to His will? Good answers. We never know exactly how God will bless our obedience of faith, but God will bless. How did God bless the Israelites in our Bible story? Right, the Israelites were able to defeat the city of Ai.

I have enjoyed our time together today. I hope you all will come back next week so we can explore another Bible story about Joshua and the Israelites as they conquer the promised land.

After I close in prayer, watch your small group leader for the signal to march to your small group.

Close in prayer. Ask God to help boys and girls remember today's big picture question each time they are faced with the choice of whether or not to obey in faith. Thank God for sending Jesus, the only perfectly obedient One, to die for our sins.

Dismiss to small groups

The Gospel: God's Plan for Me

Ask kids if they have ever heard the word *gospel*. Clarify that the word *gospel* means "good news." It is the message about Christ, the kingdom of God, and salvation. Use the following guide to share the gospel with kids.

God rules. Explain to kids that the Bible tells us God created everything, and He is in charge of everything. Invite a volunteer to read Genesis 1:1 from the Bible. Read Revelation 4:11 or Colossians 1:16-17 aloud and explain what these verses mean.

We sinned. Tell kids that since the time of Adam and Eve, everyone has chosen to disobey God. (Romans 3:23) The Bible calls this sin. Because God is holy, God cannot be around sin. Sin separates us from God and deserves God's punishment of death. (Romans 6:23)

God provided. Choose a child to read John 3:16 aloud. Say that God sent His Son, Jesus, the perfect solution to our sin problem, to rescue us from the punishment we deserve. It's something we, as sinners, could never earn on our own. Jesus alone saves us. Read and explain Ephesians 2:8-9.

Jesus gives. Share with kids that Jesus lived a perfect life, died on the cross for our sins, and rose again. Because Jesus gave up His life for us, we can be welcomed into God's family for eternity. This is the best gift ever! Read Romans 5:8; 2 Corinthians 5:21; or 1 Peter 3:18.

We respond. Tell kids that they can respond to Jesus. Read Romans 10:9-10,13. Review these aspects of our response: Believe in your heart that Jesus alone saves you through what He's already done on the cross. Repent, turning from self and sin to Jesus. Tell God and others that your faith is in Jesus.

Offer to talk with any child who is interested in responding to Jesus.

Small Group LEADER

Session Title: The Defeat of Ai
Bible Passage: Joshua 8
Big Picture Question: What does God do when we obey Him? God blesses people who obey Him in faith.
Key Passage: Joshua 24:15
Unit Christ Connection: Joshua was a representation of Christ, leading the Israelites to victory in overcoming Canaan as Jesus leads us to victory in overcoming the world.

- Bibles, 1 per kid
- Small Group Visual Pack

Bible story review & Bible skills (10 minutes)

Review the timeline in the small group visual pack. Remind kids of the Israelites' experience the first time they tried to conquer Ai.

Forms pairs or trios. Assign each group a Scripture reference. Groups will form a freeze frame or statue pose based on the Scripture. The other kids will guess which part of the story is being depicted. After every team has had a turn, lead the kids to stand in the correct order of the Bible story and form their freeze frames once more. Suggested Scripture references:

- Joshua 8:3 – Joshua sent troops to attack Ai.
- Joshua 8:14 – The king of Ai went out to fight.
- Joshua 8:15 – The Israelites pretended to retreat.
- Joshua 8:18 – Joshua held out his sword.
- Joshua 8:19 – The Israelites ambushed Ai.
- Joshua 8:22 – The people of Ai were trapped.
- Joshua 8:30 – Joshua built an altar to the Lord.
- Joshua 8:34 – Joshua read the words of the law.

Say • *What does God do when we obey Him? God blesses people who obey Him in faith.*

- Because of Christ, we are in _____ standing with

God. *(Because of Christ, we are in right standing with God. We are victorious over our enemies because of our faith in Christ. [Romans 8:37])*

If you choose to review with boys and girls how to become a Christian, explain that kids are welcome to speak with you or another teacher if they have questions.

- **God rules.** God created and is in charge of everything. (Gen. 1:1; Rev. 4:11; Col. 1:16-17)
- **We sinned.** Since Adam and Eve, everyone has chosen to disobey God. (Rom. 3:23; 6:23)
- **God provided.** God sent His Son Jesus to rescue us from the punishment we deserve. (John 3:16; Eph. 2:8-9)
- **Jesus gives.** Jesus lived a perfect life, died on the cross for our sins, and rose again so we can be welcomed into God's family. (Rom. 5:8; 2 Cor. 5:21; 1 Pet. 3:18)
- **We respond.** Believe that Jesus alone saves you. Repent. Tell God that your faith is in Jesus. (Rom. 10:9-10,13)

Key passage activity (5 minutes)

Lead kids to use the key passage to create a victory cheer or chant. You may choose to allow kids to use only a section of the key passage in the victory chant.

Say • In a couple of weeks we will hear the Bible story that our key passage comes from. Our key passage highlights the choice the Israelites had to make again and again. They could follow God, or they could follow a false god. We have the same choice. We can follow God, or we can follow someone or something else. The Bible is clear on what happens when we follow anything other than God. Idolatry is a sin.

Option: Guide preteens to locate and read Romans 8:37. For more context, you may wish to guide preteens to read Romans 8:34-39. Help them understand that God promises each Christian victory over his enemies.

• Key Passage Poster (enhanced CD)

Tip: If any kids have already memorized the key passage, challenge them to also memorize Joshua 24:14 or Joshua 24:16.

Activity choice (10 minutes)

Option 1: Pat, pat, clap, clap

Guide kids to sit in a circle and create a rhythm with you. Create a rhythm by patting your legs twice and clapping your hands together twice. Maintain a pat, pat, clap, clap pattern as you play. As you continue the pattern, allow kids to take turns naming one way God has blessed them. Offer your own suggestion last. If a kid hasn't mentioned God sending His Son, Jesus, to die on the cross, be sure to mention it. To make the game more complicated, ask each kid to name all the previous answers before providing her answer.

Say • The Israelites faced another battle in today's Bible story as they worked to conquer the promised land. ***What does God do when we obey Him? God blesses people who obey Him in faith.***

• Because of Christ, we are in _____ standing with God. *(Because of Christ, we are in right standing with God. We are victorious over our enemies because of our faith in Christ. [Romans 8:37])*

Option 2: Balloon battle

- balloons
- slips of paper
- pen
- Bibles
- tape

Prior to class, write some of God's blessings on small slips of paper and drop each paper inside a balloon. Inflate the balloons. For an extra challenge, inflate some balloons without paper inside. Tape a line down the room.

Form two groups. When you give the signal, groups may pop as many balloons as possible to collect the slips of paper. Once the kids pop all the balloons, ask each group to read the Scripture reference provided and share what blessing the verse describes.

Suggested blessing verses:

• Psalm 21:6 (God's presence, joy)

- Psalm 46:1 (help in times of trouble, strength)
- Psalm 54:4 (God's help)
- Psalm 68:19 (salvation, bearing our burdens)
- Psalm 84:11 (grace, glory, and good)
- Psalm 94:19 (comfort, joy)
- John 3:16 (love, eternal life)
- John 14:27 (peace)
- Ephesians 1:7 (redemption, forgiveness)
- 1 Peter 2:10 (mercy)

Say • To bless someone is to provide someone with something good. God provided the Israelites with a victory in today's Bible story because they obeyed Him in faith. ***What does God do when we obey Him? God blesses people who obey Him in faith.***

Journal and prayer (5 minutes)

- pencils
- journals
- Bibles
- Journal Page, 1 per kid (enhanced CD)
- "Books of the Bible Match" activity page, 1 per kid
- multiple sets of markers, crayons, or colored pencils in the following colors: red, blue, purple, yellow, and green

Tip: Allow kids to reference the Books of the Bible chart in the back of the activity pages book.

Allow kids to write a prayer to God on their journal page. Kids may write a prayer request, a thanksgiving, a confession, a praise, and so forth.

Say • ***What does God do when we obey Him? God blesses people who obey Him in faith.***

If time allows, assist boys and girls in completing the activity page, "Books of the Bible Match." Teach kids who need assistance how to use the table of contents page in the front of the Bible to help. Explain to boys and girls that remembering the number of books in each Old Testament division is as easy as remembering this code: 5, 12, 5, 5, 12.

- books of Law: 5 books
- books of History: 12 books
- books of Poetry and Wisdom: 5 books
- Major Prophets: 5 books
- Minor Prophets: 12 books

Teacher BIBLE STUDY

The Gibeonites were a deceitful people. They lied to Joshua about where they were from because they did not want Israel to attack them. (See Joshua 9:3-6.) Even though God had warned Joshua not to make treaties with anyone (Deut. 7:2), the Gibeonites convinced Joshua to make a peace treaty with them. When Joshua found out he had been tricked, he was mad.

When the king of Jerusalem heard how Joshua had captured Ai and made peace with Gibeon, he was very afraid because Gibeon was a great city. The king of Jerusalem called to the four other kings in the land, and the kings formed a coalition and made war against Gibeon.

The men of Gibeon sent word to Joshua and said, "Please come help us!" God reassured Joshua that He would be with him in defending the Gibeonites.

God fought for the Israelites! He threw the five kings' armies into confusion. While the armies fled, God threw down large hailstones from heaven, and they died. God killed more men with hailstones than the Israelites killed with their swords.

Joshua and the Israelites were still in battle, but time was running out. It would get dark soon. So Joshua prayed to God: "Sun, stand still over Gibeon." God made it happen. The sun stood still for almost a full day. The Israelites won the battle and returned to their camp.

What an exciting story! Joshua's name, which means, "Yahweh is salvation" testifies to the Lord's saving hand. God fought for the Israelites and made them victorious over their enemies. This story points ahead to another time when God saved His people in an even greater way. God sent His Son Jesus to fight the battle against sin and death. Jesus died, taking the punishment for sin, and then rose again triumphantly. Because of our faith in Jesus, we too are victorious over sin and death.

Older Kids BIBLE STUDY OVERVIEW

Session Title: The Day the Sun Stood Still
Bible Passage: Joshua 10:1-15
Big Picture Question: What does God do when we pray? God answers
the prayers of His people and saves them.
Key Passage: Joshua 24:15
Unit Christ Connection: Joshua was a representation of Christ, leading
the Israelites to victory in overcoming Canaan as Jesus leads us to
victory in overcoming the world.

Small Group Opening

Large Group Leader

Small Group Leader

The BIBLE STORY

The Day the Sun Stood Still
Joshua 10:1-15

Joshua and the Israelites had defeated Jericho and Ai (AY igh). They made peace with their neighbors, the people of Gibeon (GIB ih uhn) because the Gibeonites tricked them. The land they were in was ruled by five kings. The kings did not love God or worship Him. The king of Jerusalem heard what the Israelites did to Jericho and Ai, and how the Israelites had made peace with the Gibeonites. He was very afraid because Gibeon was a great city, and all its men were warriors. Now the Gibeonites and the Israelites were on the same side!

The king of Jerusalem called to the other four kings in the land. He said to them, "Come with me and help me attack Gibeon because it has made peace with Joshua and the people of Israel." So the five kings joined forces and went up with all their armies and camped outside Gibeon and started a war against Gibeon.

The men of Gibeon sent a message to Joshua: "Help us! Save us! All the kings who live in this land are at war with us." So Joshua and his whole army went to Gibeon to help them fight.

The LORD said to Joshua, "Do not be afraid of them, for I have handed them over to you. Not one of them will be able to stand against you." Joshua knew the Israelites would have to fight, but he depended on God to help them win.

Joshua and his army marched all night from where they were staying and they surprised the five kings' armies. The LORD confused the armies of the kings. As the Israelites fought, God helped them kill their enemies. The kings' armies fled. The LORD threw huge hailstones from the sky, killing the men as they ran away. More men died from the hailstones than the Israelites killed with their swords.

The battle was not over. Joshua needed more time to fight before the sun went down. On that day, Joshua prayed to God where all of the Israelites could hear him. He said, "Sun, stand still over Gibeon, and moon, over the valley of Aijalon (A juh lahn)." The sun stood still and the moon stopped until Israel and Gibeon defeated their enemies. The sun stopped in the middle of the day and did not set for almost a full day.

There has been no day like it before or since. It was a day when God listened to the voice of man and fought for the Israelites. When the battle was over, Joshua and all his army returned to where they were camping at Gilgal.

Christ Connection: Joshua's name means "Yahweh is salvation." God fought for Joshua and the Israelites, saving them and giving them victory over their enemies. God brought us salvation by sending His Son Jesus to die on the cross, giving us victory over sin and death.

Small Group OPENING

Session Title: The Day the Sun Stood Still
Bible Passage: Joshua 10:1-15
Big Picture Question: What does God do when we pray? God answers the prayers of His people and saves them.
Key Passage: Joshua 24:15
Unit Christ Connection: Joshua was a representation of Christ, leading the Israelites to victory in overcoming Canaan as Jesus leads us to victory in overcoming the world.

Welcome time

Greet each kid as he or she arrives. Use this time to collect the offering, fill out attendance sheets, and help new kids connect to your group. Invite kids to share a time they remember God answering one of their prayers.

- "Did You Know?" activity page, 1 per kid
- pencils

Activity page (5 minutes)

Help kids decode the statements on the activity page, "Did You Know?"

Say • Did you know all of those facts about hail, the sun, and the moon? Did you know what Joshua's name meant? Does anyone remember any other Bible stories about hail or the sun or the moon? What about other stories about Joshua?

Pause for kids to answer the questions as they complete the activity page. Allow kids to share about other Bible stories your class has studied or about Bible stories they may have heard elsewhere that involve hail, the sun, the moon, or Joshua.

Say • Hail, the sun, the moon, and the meaning of Joshua's name are all a part of today's Bible story and Christ connection.

• cotton balls, at least
5–10 per kid

Tip: The more cotton
balls, the better.

Session starter (10 minutes)

Option 1: Hailstone game

Divide the room in two sections. Scatter cotton balls evenly on each side. Form two teams. Inform teams that the cotton balls represent hailstones in today's game. Explain that the goal of the game is for each team to toss all the hailstones from its section into the other team's section. Anyone who is hit by a hailstone may not toss a hailstone for 10 seconds. Hailstones cannot be purposely thrown at players.

Say •Hailstones are an important factor in today's Bible story. Once again, the Israelites must fight another battle in the conquest of the promised land. We will see what happened to the Israelites during the battle against five enemy kings and their armies.

• 2 long taped lines
on the floor several
feet apart

Options:
You may choose
for groups to play
each round with
a different type
of walking (on
knees, sideways, on
tiptoes, on one leg,
small steps).

Two people can
share the role of
caller. One will say
"go" and the other
will say "stop."

Option 2: Stop and go groups

Form pairs or trios and guide groups to link arms. Ask groups to form a line standing along the first taped line. Select one kid to be the caller. The caller will stand several feet in front of the line of kids. With his back to the other kids, the caller will give the command, "go."

The groups will begin walking forward toward the other taped line. The caller may give the command "stop" at any time and all kids must stop moving. If a kid moves after the command "stop," her group must return to the start line. One person from the first group to cross the taped line becomes the new caller.

Say •In our Bible story today, God stopped something very important from moving because someone prayed. When it stopped moving, it helped the Israelites.

Transition to large group

Large Group LEADER

Session Title: The Day the Sun Stood Still
Bible Passage: Joshua 10:1-15
Big Picture Question: What does God do when we pray? God answers the prayers of His people and saves them.
Key Passage: Joshua 24:15
Unit Christ Connection: Joshua was a representation of Christ, leading the Israelites to victory in overcoming Canaan as Jesus leads us to victory in overcoming the world.

• countdown video

Countdown

Show the countdown video as your kids arrive, and set it to end as large group time begins.

• sunglasses, several pairs including some silly options
• bag

Option: Select volunteers to come to the stage and wear the sunglasses. Kids may vote as you hold your hand over the head of each volunteer.

Introduce the session (3 minutes)

[Large Group Leader enters the room looking through a bag full of sunglasses.]

Leader • Hello, friends! I'm glad to see you are back at our old fort. I heard that it was going to be very sunny at our fort today, so I am trying to find the perfect pair of sunglasses.

Let's play a game. I will try on a pair and if you think they are sunglasses I need, clap your hands and stop your feet to make as much noise as you can. After I try all of them on, the pair that receives the most noise response from you will be the winner.

Try on several pairs and allow kids to indicate their favorite pair for you to wear.

Leader • Wow. This pair of sunglasses will really help keep the sun out of my eyes today at our old fort. Who created the sun? Right! God created everything! Have you ever been playing outside and had to stop and go inside because the sun set and it was dark? When I was your age, I would play outside but when the sun set, I couldn't see very well to keep playing. We didn't have a lot of streetlights in my neighborhood. When it was dark, you just couldn't see very well.

If you were a soldier back when our fort was new, would you want to fight a battle at night, or during the day? Remember back then, they didn't have flashlights and bright lamps. They didn't have any electricity. People had to carry torches. Would a torch give you enough light to fight a battle? No. Would it be hard to hold a torch and fight a battle? Yes. Back in the days of our old fort, when it got dark, you had to stop fighting a battle.

• Timeline Map

Timeline map (1 minute)

Leader • We've been studying the Israelites and their battles to conquer the promised land. Someone name one of the cities the Israelites conquered. The Israelites conquered both Jericho and Ai.

Indicate the Bible stories for Jericho and Ai on the timeline.

Leader • Do you think the Israelites needed light to conquer the cities in the promised land? Yes. They definitely needed light. Light is so important in today's Bible story that someone prayed about it. Before we open our Bibles, you need to know the big picture question.

Big picture question (1 minute)

Tip: A kid may occasionally know the right answer to the big picture question. Always be encouraging about kids' responses without revealing if a kid has provided the correct answer.

Leader • *What does God do when we pray?* What do you think God does when you pray?

Select a couple of kids to share their responses.

Leader • You all have very interesting answers. Anytime we have a question about God, we can look for the answer in the Bible. Our Bible story is in Joshua 10, so everyone find the Book of Joshua in your Bible. Remember it is the book before Judges and the book after Deuteronomy.

• "The Day the Sun Stood Still" video
• Bibles
• Bible Story Picture Slide or Poster (enhanced CD)
• Big Picture Question Slide or Poster (enhanced CD)

Tell the Bible story (9 minutes)

Open your Bible to Joshua 10 and tell the Bible story in your own words, or show the Bible story video "The Day the Sun Stood Still."

Leader • What happened when Joshua prayed to God? The Bible says God heard Joshua's prayer and said yes to Joshua's request. The Israelites had enough light to finish the battle and defeat the five kings and their armies.

Our big picture question is, ***What does God do when we pray?*** The Bible reveals that the answer is, ***God answers the prayers of His people and saves them.*** God answers the prayers of His people in different ways. Does God always say yes when we pray? No. Sometimes God knows that the only way to save us is to say *no* to our prayer. Sometimes God knows we need to wait awhile before He says yes to our prayer. We don't see the big picture of our lives, but God does. He knows everything that will happen in our lives. He knows what is best for us. Sometimes what is best for us is for God to say no to our prayer. That can be really hard for us to understand. We need to remember that God loves us, and His plans for us are perfect. We may not get the answer we want, but God will answer the prayers of His people. We have to trust Him even when He answers our prayers in a way we don't like. ***What does God do when we pray? God answers the prayers of His people and saves them.***

Does anyone remember what Joshua's name means? Joshua's name means "Yahweh is salvation." Under Joshua's leadership, the Israelites often experienced God's salvation as they fought battles to conquer the promised land. God provided the Israelites with victory in many battles.

God has provided salvation for us as well. God sent His Son to live on earth. Jesus lived without sinning; He was perfect. He paid the price for our sin by dying on the cross. God raised Him from the dead three days later. Jesus defeated sin and death. Because Jesus defeated sin and death, we can have victory over sin and death when we confess our sin and trust Jesus as Lord and Savior.

• Bibles for small group leaders

The Gospel: God's Plan for Me (optional)

Use the suggested Scriptures and guide provided to tell kids how to become a Christian. Ask some of the small group leaders to read aloud the suggested Scriptures when you indicate. Explain to kids how they can respond, and have counselors available to speak with kids who have questions or are ready to become a Christian.

• "Our God" song

Sing (5 minutes)

Leader • Stand with me and sing to our great God. He is our salvation and has provided the way for us to have victory over sin and death through Jesus. God is worthy of all glory and honor.

Sing the unit theme song, "Our God."

• "Unit 8 Session 5" discussion starter video

Discussion starter video (5 minutes)

Leader • Name some of the times you pray.

Select five or six kids to respond.

Leader • What about when you hear something bad or upsetting has happened? Do you pray, or do you continue what you are doing? Watch this video and we'll talk about it afterward.

Show the "Unit 8 Session 5" discussion starter video.

Leader • What could the kid do in that situation? Have any of you ever been in a similar situation? What did you do? Thanks for sharing. Who remembers our big picture question? *What does God do when we pray? God answers the prayers of His people and saves them.* We can pray to God anytime, anywhere, no matter what.

• Key Passage Slide or Poster (enhanced CD)
• "Choose for Yourself" song

Tip: If you have kids who have already memorized the key passage, challenge them to also memorize Joshua 24:14 or Joshua 24:16.

Key passage (4 minutes)

Leader • We only have one more week to memorize our key passage. If you are having trouble memorizing it, ask your parents or a guardian to help you. Who did Joshua and his family serve? Joshua and his family served Yahweh, the Lord! I pray that you will serve the Lord. Sing our key passage song with me.

Lead kids to read the key passage together. Sing "Choose for Yourself."

Prayer (2 minutes)

Leader • It has been a beautiful, sunny day here at our old fort. God answered Joshua's prayer. Can you imagine how sunny it was on that day? *What does God do when we pray? God answers the prayers of His people and saves them.* Remember, God loves you and His plans for you are perfect. He will answer your prayers in the way that is best for you. The next time you see the sun shining, remember how God answered the prayer of Joshua and saved the Israelites. After I pray, watch your small group leader for the signal to go to small group.

Close in prayer.

Dismiss to small groups

The Gospel: God's Plan for Me

Ask kids if they have ever heard the word *gospel*. Clarify that the word *gospel* means "good news." It is the message about Christ, the kingdom of God, and salvation. Use the following guide to share the gospel with kids.

God rules. Explain to kids that the Bible tells us God created everything, and He is in charge of everything. Invite a volunteer to read Genesis 1:1 from the Bible. Read Revelation 4:11 or Colossians 1:16-17 aloud and explain what these verses mean.

We sinned. Tell kids that since the time of Adam and Eve, everyone has chosen to disobey God. (Romans 3:23) The Bible calls this sin. Because God is holy, God cannot be around sin. Sin separates us from God and deserves God's punishment of death. (Romans 6:23)

God provided. Choose a child to read John 3:16 aloud. Say that God sent His Son, Jesus, the perfect solution to our sin problem, to rescue us from the punishment we deserve. It's something we, as sinners, could never earn on our own. Jesus alone saves us. Read and explain Ephesians 2:8-9.

Jesus gives. Share with kids that Jesus lived a perfect life, died on the cross for our sins, and rose again. Because Jesus gave up His life for us, we can be welcomed into God's family for eternity. This is the best gift ever! Read Romans 5:8; 2 Corinthians 5:21; or 1 Peter 3:18.

We respond. Tell kids that they can respond to Jesus. Read Romans 10:9-10,13. Review these aspects of our response: Believe in your heart that Jesus alone saves you through what He's already done on the cross. Repent, turning from self and sin to Jesus. Tell God and others that your faith is in Jesus.

Offer to talk with any child who is interested in responding to Jesus.

Small Group LEADER

Session Title: The Day the Sun Stood Still
Bible Passage: Joshua 10:1-15
Big Picture Question: What does God do when we pray? God answers the prayers of His people and saves them.
Key Passage: Joshua 24:15
Unit Christ Connection: Joshua was a representation of Christ, leading the Israelites to victory in overcoming Canaan as Jesus leads us to victory in overcoming the world.

- Bibles, 1 per kid
- Small Group Visual Pack

Bible story review & Bible skills (10 minutes)

Allow boys and girls to retell the Bible story. Select a kid to begin the story. Every time you say the phrase, "sun stand still," the current speaker must stop immediately and select another kid to continue the story. Guide kids to reference the Bible story in Joshua 10 if needed.

Say • *What does God do when we pray? God answers the prayers of His people and saves them.*

• Who gives us victory over sin and death? (*God brought us salvation by sending His Son Jesus to die on the cross, giving us victory over sin and death.*)

If you choose to review with boys and girls how to become a Christian, explain that kids are welcome to speak with you or another teacher if they have questions.

- **God rules.** God created and is in charge of everything. (Gen. 1:1; Rev. 4:11; Col. 1:16-17)

- **We sinned.** Since Adam and Eve, everyone has chosen to disobey God. (Rom. 3:23; 6:23)

- **God provided.** God sent His Son Jesus to rescue us from the punishment we deserve. (John 3:16; Eph. 2:8-9)

- **Jesus gives.** Jesus lived a perfect life, died on the

cross for our sins, and rose again so we can be welcomed into God's family. (Rom. 5:8; 2 Cor. 5:21; 1 Pet. 3:18)

- **We respond.** Believe that Jesus alone saves you. Repent. Tell God that your faith is in Jesus. (Rom. 10:9-10,13)

Review the timeline in the small group visual pack. Remind kids of God's promise to Abraham to bring his descendants back to the land. (Genesis 12:6-7; 15:18-21; 17:7-8) The Israelites fought to conquer the land God spoke about in His promise to Abraham.

Key passage activity (5 minutes)

- Key Passage Poster (enhanced CD)
- ball, yellow or orange preferred

Allow kids to toss the "sun" to one another. Each time a player catches the sun, he must say the next word in the key passage. Play more than once, allowing kids to increase the speed of the game in the later round(s).

Say • Next week is our last week to study this key passage. If you are having trouble memorizing the passage, try breaking it up into smaller sections and work on one section each day.

Activity choice (10 minutes)

- cloth tape measure
- construction paper sun, 1 per team
- tape
- numbered cube or spinner

Option 1: Setting sun game

Lead kids to form teams. For each team, tape a paper sun at the bottom of a wall. Each team will have the opportunity to answer a review question. If the question is answered correctly, a team member may roll a numbered cube to determine how many inches the team may move its sun up on the wall.

After the teams answer all the questions, determine which team's sun has risen the highest in the sky (the highest on the wall).

Tip: Tape the cloth tape measure to the wall, beginning at the floor.

Option: Allow kids to play as individuals or pairs. Create more questions to allow individuals or pairs to answer more than one question.

1. How many enemy kings attacked Gibeon? (*five, Josh. 10:5*)

2. Whom did the Gibeonites ask to come save them? (*Joshua and the Israelites, Josh. 10:6*)

3. When did Joshua and his army march to Gibeon? (*They marched all night, Josh. 10:9*)

4. What did God throw down from the sky to help defeat the enemy armies? (*hailstones, Josh. 10:11*)

5. Who prayed to God for help during the battle? (*Joshua, Josh. 10:12*)

6. What did Joshua pray? (*He asked for the sun to stand still over Gibeon and the moon over the valley of Aijalon, Josh. 10:12*)

7. How did God answer Joshua's prayer? (*He allowed the sun to stay and provide light for the Israelites to defeat the enemy armies, Josh. 10:13*)

8. Who fought for the Israelites? (*God, Josh. 10:14*)

9. ***What does God do when we pray? God answers the prayers of His people and saves them.***

10. How did God bring us salvation? (*God brought us salvation by sending His Son Jesus to die on the cross, giving us victory over sin and death.*)

• white fabric rectangles or handkerchiefs
• permanent markers or fabric markers
• ribbon, 2 pieces per kid
• hole punch or scissors
• paper

Option 2: Victory fort banner

Lead kids to create a banner to celebrate the victory the Israelites had on the day the sun stood still. Guide kids to include a sun or hailstones on their banner. Kids may wish to print a phrase from today's Bible story, such as *Do not be afraid*, or part of the big picture answer on the banner. Help kids use the hole punch or scissors to create two holes in the top of the banner. Thread ribbon through each hole and tie the ends to create a loop for hanging the banner.

Older Kids Bible Study Leader Guide
Unit 8 • Session 5
© 2012 LifeWay Christian Resources

Say • *What does God do when we pray? God answers the prayers of His people and saves them.*

• What did Joshua pray? (*Joshua asked for the sun to stand still over Gibeon and the moon over the valley of Aijalon, Josh. 10:12*)

• How did God answer Joshua's prayer? (*He allowed the sun to stay and provide light for the Israelites to defeat the enemy armies, Josh. 10:13*)

• pencils
• journals
• Bibles
• Journal Page,
  1 per kid (enhanced CD)
• "Prayer Shields" activity page,
  1 per kid

Journal and prayer (5 minutes)

Ask kids to look through their journals at the prayer requests they have recorded. Guide kids to write a prayer thanking God for the requests they have seen answered already. Lead kids to write down any new prayer requests. Select a volunteer to close the group in prayer.

Say • *What does God do when we pray? God answers the prayers of His people and saves them.*

As time allows, lead kids to complete the activity page, "Prayer Shields."

Teacher BIBLE STUDY

Joshua was "getting on in years" (Josh. 23:1). So Joshua gathered up all the people of Israel to give an exhortation.

First, Joshua reminded them that God had fought for His people, and He kept every single one of His promises. (Josh. 23:14) Joshua wanted the people to remember and to live their lives based on what they knew to be true about God: God can be trusted. He is good, and He is faithful.

In Joshua 23:6, Joshua issued a challenge: "Be very strong and continue obeying all that is written in the book of the law of Moses." Reading, studying, and obeying God's Word is a mark of belief in God. Joshua reminded the people that they were successful over their enemies because of their obedience to God.

Finally, Joshua gave the Israelites a warning. Just as all the good things God promised had been fulfilled, so would all the bad things He promised if the Israelites disobeyed Him. (See Josh. 23:12-13,15.)

Joshua gathered the people at the place where God had made a promise to Abraham. (See Gen. 12:6-7.) Joshua reminded the leaders of the past—from the birth of Isaac to Israel's escape from Egypt. Joshua said, "Choose for yourselves today the one you will worship … As for me and my family, we will worship Yahweh" (Josh. 24:15).

The Israelites had a choice: Continue to worship God or choose to serve other gods. In response to God's faithfulness to His promises, the Israelites renewed their covenant to be faithful to the LORD.

As you share the story of Joshua's legacy with kids, point them to a greater legacy found in Jesus Christ. After Christ's resurrection, He sent His disciples out to tell the nations about Him. Jesus calls all people who trust in Him to tell others about Him.

Older Kids BIBLE STUDY OVERVIEW

Session Title: Joshua's Final Encouragement
Bible Passage: Joshua 23:1–24:28
Big Picture Question: How can we show we love God? We can serve, worship, and obey God.
Key Passage: Joshua 24:15
Unit Christ Connection: Joshua was a representation of Christ, leading the Israelites to victory in overcoming Canaan as Jesus leads us to victory in overcoming the world.

Small Group Opening

Large Group Leader

Small Group Leader

The BIBLE STORY

Joshua's Final Encouragement
Joshua 23:1–24:28

Many years had passed since Joshua and the Israelites had defeated Jericho, Ai (AY igh), and the kings of the land. God allowed the Israelites to rest from battles against their enemies. Joshua was getting old. He gathered all the people of Israel because he had some important things to say to them. Joshua said, "You have seen everything the LORD your God has done—He has fought your battles for you. All of the land that remains will be yours too. God will push back the people who live there and move them out of your sight. You will possess that land, just as the LORD your God promised you."

"Therefore," Joshua continued, "be careful to obey everything that is in the book of the law of Moses. Do not turn aside from it; do not mix with the nations in this land or worship their gods. Cling to God, just as you have done. God fights for you! Be very careful, then, to love the LORD your God. If you disobey God, He will no longer help you win these battles. In fact, you will die here if you disobey Him."

Joshua spoke more to the Israelites. He said, "I am going to die soon. All of you know in your hearts and souls that God has kept every one of His promises. But know for certain that if you disobey God, He will keep His promise to bring bad things upon you, and you will die in this land He has given to you."

Joshua reminded all the people about the things God had done for them in the past. Joshua reminded them of everything from when God called Abraham and gave him a son, Isaac, to when God gave Isaac two sons, Jacob and Esau. He reminded them that Jacob's children went to Egypt, where God sent Moses and Aaron. Joshua told the people about how God had rescued the Israelites from the Egyptians, bringing them safely across the Red Sea and saving them from the Egyptians who were chasing them. Joshua reminded them of the many battles they had fought and won because God was fighting for them. God had done so many great things for His people!

Joshua commanded the people, "Fear the LORD and worship Him. If you don't want to worship God, choose to worship the gods your fathers worshiped. As for me and my family, we will worship Yahweh."

The people replied, "We will certainly not abandon the LORD to worship other gods! We know how much God has done for us, and we love Him!"

Joshua warned the people, "If you do abandon God to worship other gods, God will turn against you and harm you. He will destroy you, after all of the good things He has done for you!"

"No!" the people replied. "We will worship Yahweh!"

On that day, Joshua made a covenant with the people. He wrote it down in the book of the law of God. He also took a large stone and set it up under an oak tree next to the sanctuary of the LORD.

"You see this stone," Joshua said. "It will be a reminder of your duty to serve the LORD, who fulfilled every promise in bringing you into this land." Then Joshua sent the people away, each man went to the land he had inherited.

Christ Connection: As Joshua prepared for his own death, he left behind a legacy of obedience to God. After Jesus' death and resurrection, He appeared to the disciples and left them with a legacy: to make disciples of all nations, baptizing them in the name of the Father and of the Son and of the Holy Spirit, teaching them to obey everything Jesus commanded. (Matthew 28:19-20)

Small Group OPENING

Session Title: Joshua's Final Encouragement
Bible Passage: Joshua 23:1–24:28
Big Picture Question: How can we show we love God? We can serve, worship, and obey God.
Key Passage: Joshua 24:15
Unit Christ Connection: Joshua was a representation of Christ, leading the Israelites to victory in overcoming Canaan as Jesus leads us to victory in overcoming the world.

Welcome time

Greet each kid as he or she arrives. Use this time to collect the offering, fill out attendance sheets, and help new kids connect to your group. Invite kids to share if anyone said or did something that encouraged them during the week. Invite kids to share the key passage from memory if they can.

Activity page (5 minutes)

- "Number and Letter Puzzle" activity page, 1 per kid
- pencils
- Bibles, 1 per kid

Assist kids in decoding the activity page, "Number and Letter Puzzle," to review the history of the Israelite nation.

Say • God promised Abraham that he would have many descendants. Abraham's descendants became the nation of Israel, God's chosen people. The Israelites had almost conquered the promised land. It was time for the people to go live in the land they had been given. Listen closely today to what Joshua told the people about loving and following God.

Session starter (10 minutes)

Option 1: Star hunt

- paper stars or glow-in-the-dark plastic stars, 29 or 35
- permanent marker

Write previous Bible story titles or descriptions on stars. Challenge kids to arrange the stories in chronological order.

- timer
- Write on each star the title of a Bible story beginning with *God Created the World and People*. If you choose to include the Christmas and Easter stories, you will need 35 stars. If you omit the Christmas and Easter stories, you will need 29 stars.

Option: Use the Small Group Visual Pack as your guide.

- markers
- pens or pencils
- heavyweight paper
- copy paper
- card envelopes
- letter envelopes
- stickers
- Bibles, 1 per kid

Tip: Help kids locate the Scriptures in the Bible. Discuss what each one says and how it can encourage someone.

Guide kids to play again, but allow them to set a time goal they want to attempt. As kids arrange the pieces, time them to see if they reach their goal. Continue rounds of the game with new time goals as time allows.

Say • In today's Bible story, Joshua reminded the people of all God had done for them. Several of the Bible stories Joshua mentioned are stories we have studied.

• Which of these stories is your favorite? Why?

Option 2: Encouraging words

Say • What are some ways we can love God? One way we can love God is through helping others. What are some ways we can help others? One way we can help other people is to encourage them to remember Scripture, God's Word. You are going to make a card or write a letter encouraging someone to remember a verse of Scripture. I have some suggestions, but you may choose the verse you want to use.

Guide kids to write an encouraging note to a teacher, neighbor, family member, or friend. Kids may make more than one note if time allows. Encourage kids to include Scripture in their encouraging note. (Suggested Scriptures: Psalm 8:1; Psalm 29:11; Proverbs 3:5; 2 Corinthians 5:17; Philippians 4:6-7; Colossians 3:23)

Say • Why it is important to encourage others to remember Scripture? Our Bible story marks the end of a season of time in the lives of the Israelites. Joshua, their leader as they conquered the promised land, was at the end of his life. Today we will hear some of his final words of encouragement to the Israelites.

Transition to large group

Large Group LEADER

Session Title: Joshua's Final Encouragement
Bible Passage: Joshua 23:1–24:28
Big Picture Question: How can we show we love God? We can serve, worship, and obey God.
Key Passage: Joshua 24:15
Unit Christ Connection: Joshua was a representation of Christ, leading the Israelites to victory in overcoming Canaan as Jesus leads us to victory in overcoming the world.

Countdown

• countdown video

Show the countdown video as your kids arrive, and set it to end as large group time begins.

Introduce the session (3 minutes)

[Large Group Leader enters and speaks in an old scratchy voice. Move slowly and exaggerate. Drag out the "left, right, left" words to match the slow pace of the physical movement.]

Leader • Left, left, left, right, left. That's all the marching I could handle if I were over 100 years old. Do you want to try marching like you are over 100 years old? You do. Stand up. On the count of three, everyone march. One, two, three. Left, left, left, right, left. Now everyone sit back down.

Can you imagine being that old? I wouldn't want to be a solider at this old fort if I were over 100 years old. Someone in our Bible story today was over 100 years old. He had some important words to share with the Israelites. Anyone want to guess who I am talking about? Joshua! Imagine all the things you could experience in 100 years. Think about all the battles Joshua led the Israelites in.

We've talked about some of them, but not all of the battles. Conquering the promised land was a big job, but who fought for the Israelites? Who helped them win the battles? God! God's covenant with the Israelites promised them that He would protect, guide, and sustain them if they obeyed God and worshiped Him. The covenant God made with the Israelites is an important part of today's Bible story. Join me in looking at our timeline map.

Timeline map (2 minutes)

• Timeline Map

Tip: If you have a large room, ask a volunteer to stand by the timeline map with you.

Leader • I am going to point to a Bible story picture and ask a volunteer to tell me what story it is.

Review the Bible stories from this unit. If you have extra time, review stories from past units.

Leader • Great job! I am glad to see and hear that you have been really listening each week as we explore the big picture of God's story. Each of the Bible stories we have studied was a part of God's plan to send Jesus to rescue us from sin. All of the stories are connected to each other. When we study them in order, we can see how God's plan unfolded one piece at a time, one story at a time, one person at a time. And we are also a part of God's story. He has a part for each of us in His story.

Big picture question (1 minute)

Leader • Part of God's plan for us is to follow Him. When we know and love God, we are committed to Him. Our big picture question is, *How can we show we love God?* I like this big picture question because it makes me think. Where should we look to find the answer to our big picture question? We should look at the Bible. Open your Bible to Joshua 23, and we will find our big picture answer in today's Bible story.

- "Joshua's Final Encouragement" video
- Bibles
- Bible Story Picture Slide or Poster (enhanced CD)
- Big Picture Question Slide or Poster (enhanced CD)

Tell the Bible story (8 minutes)

Open your Bible to Joshua 23 and tell the Bible story in your own words, or show the Bible story video "Joshua's Final Encouragement."

Leader • Joshua loved the Israelites. He had led them for many years. He had guided them in battle. He had helped them follow God. He left a legacy of obedience to God. A *legacy* is something given to a later generation. It can be a gift, an attitude, or an example. You can leave a good legacy or a bad legacy.

Do you remember the first time we really talked about Joshua? Yes, it was a story from the Book of Numbers. Joshua and Caleb were spies who told the people they could conquer the promised land if they trusted God, but the people refused. Joshua waited 40 years to enter the promised land because the people chose to sin. Now, Joshua had led the people to enter the promised land and conquer it. The land had been divided up among all the Israelites so they knew where to live in their new home.

Joshua had seen God perform many, many miracles. Joshua remembered the price the Israelites paid when they refused to follow God. He remembered how God had saved, protected, sustained, and guided the Israelites when they obeyed Him. Joshua understood how important it was for the people to continue loving God.

Who remembers our big picture question? *How can we show we love God? We can serve, worship, and obey God.* Joshua told the people to choose whether or not they were going to be committed to loving God. His family was committed to loving God. The Israelites chose to be committed to loving God.

We also have a choice to make. *How can we show we love God? We can serve, worship, and obey God.* This is the legacy of the followers of Jesus. We can serve, worship, and obey God. We can share the gospel with people from all nations. We can teach them how to serve, worship, and obey God.

Key passage (5 minutes)

- Key Passage Slide or Poster (enhanced CD)
- "Choose for Yourself" song

Leader • Our key passage this unit is from today's Bible story. It captures a key moment in the story. Do I have any volunteers who would like to say the key passage?

Choose a couple of kids to share the key passage. Guide the two volunteers to lead the class to read the key passage together. Sing "Choose for Yourself."

The Gospel: God's Plan for Me (optional)

- Bibles

Leader • God invites us to choose Him. God loves us and sent His Son to rescue us from sin. We can receive the gift of salvation God has provided.

Explain to the boys and girls how to become a Christian. Provide kids an opportunity to respond and speak with a counselor one-on-one.

Discussion starter video (4 minutes)

- "Unit 8 Session 6" discussion starter video

Leader • What is our big picture question and answer? *How can we show we love God? We can serve, worship, and obey God.* Is it always easy to show we love God? Did the Israelites ever struggle to serve, worship, and obey God? Yes. What about us? Do we ever struggle to serve, worship, and obey God? Watch today's video and we'll talk about it.

Show the "Unit 8 Session 6" discussion starter video.

Leader • What a tough decision to make! Have any of you ever had to make a similar decision? It can be hard to choose to serve, worship, and obey God. What advice would you give? What would you do?

Remember that more than one answer may be right. Help kids verbalize what they think would be a good choice in light of today's Bible story.

Sing (5 minutes)

• "Our God" song

Tip: If time allows, you may choose to ask kids if there is a part of the song they do not understand. Explain the lyrics in question.

Leader • *How can we show we love God? We can serve, worship, and obey God.* Name some ways we can serve, worship, and obey God. All of those are good answers. What's a way we could worship right now? We can sing our unit theme song.

Lead kids to sing "Our God."

Prayer (2 minutes)

Leader • *How can we show we love God? We can serve, worship, and obey God.* Joshua left a legacy of obedience to God. He tried to lead the Israelites to always be obedient to God. Our legacy is to share the gospel with others. We are to help people understand how to serve, worship, and obey God.

This old fort sure was a nice place to visit. We learned a lot about Joshua and the Israelites. The Israelites now had the land God promised their ancestor Abraham. Next week we will discover if the Israelites continued to serve, worship, and obey God after Joshua's death. Who would be the new leader? Come back and we will find out. After I close in prayer, watch your small group leader for the signal to march to your small group.

Close in prayer.

Dismiss to small groups

The Gospel: God's Plan for Me

Ask kids if they have ever heard the word *gospel*. Clarify that the word *gospel* means "good news." It is the message about Christ, the kingdom of God, and salvation. Use the following guide to share the gospel with kids.

God rules. Explain to kids that the Bible tells us God created everything, and He is in charge of everything. Invite a volunteer to read Genesis 1:1 from the Bible. Read Revelation 4:11 or Colossians 1:16-17 aloud and explain what these verses mean.

We sinned. Tell kids that since the time of Adam and Eve, everyone has chosen to disobey God. (Romans 3:23) The Bible calls this sin. Because God is holy, God cannot be around sin. Sin separates us from God and deserves God's punishment of death. (Romans 6:23)

God provided. Choose a child to read John 3:16 aloud. Say that God sent His Son, Jesus, the perfect solution to our sin problem, to rescue us from the punishment we deserve. It's something we, as sinners, could never earn on our own. Jesus alone saves us. Read and explain Ephesians 2:8-9.

Jesus gives. Share with kids that Jesus lived a perfect life, died on the cross for our sins, and rose again. Because Jesus gave up His life for us, we can be welcomed into God's family for eternity. This is the best gift ever! Read Romans 5:8; 2 Corinthians 5:21; or 1 Peter 3:18.

We respond. Tell kids that they can respond to Jesus. Read Romans 10:9-10,13. Review these aspects of our response: Believe in your heart that Jesus alone saves you through what He's already done on the cross. Repent, turning from self and sin to Jesus. Tell God and others that your faith is in Jesus.

Offer to talk with any child who is interested in responding to Jesus.

Small Group LEADER

Session Title: Joshua's Final Encouragement
Bible Passage: Joshua 23:1–24:28
Big Picture Question: How can we show we love God? We can serve, worship, and obey God.
Key Passage: Joshua 24:15
Unit Christ Connection: Joshua was a representation of Christ, leading the Israelites to victory in overcoming Canaan as Jesus leads us to victory in overcoming the world.

- Bibles, 1 per kid
- Small Group Visual Pack
- poster board
- markers
- "Exodus to Promised Land Map" (enhanced CD)

Bible story review & Bible skills (10 minutes)

Review the journey of the Israelites by creating a large map of Egypt, Sinai, and the promised land. Help kids use the small map provided to label key cities or areas of importance to the Israelites' journey on the large map. Guide kids to use the timeline in the small group visual pack and their Bibles to identify key locations on the Israelites journey.

Suggested Scriptures:

Exodus 8:22 – Goshen (Israelites' home in Egypt)

Exodus 13:20 – Succoth, Etham (camp before Red Sea)

Exodus 16:1 – Wilderness of Sin (camp after Red Sea)

Exodus 19:1, 17-19 – Sinai (where God gave the Ten Commandments)

Numbers 13:1-3 – Wilderness of Paran (where the Israelites refused to enter the promised land)

Numbers 22:1 – plains of Moab (where Balak tried to curse the Israelites)

Joshua 3:1; 4:19 – Jordan River and Gilgal

Joshua 2:1; 6:1 – Jericho

Joshua 8:1 – Ai

Say • It was a long journey for Joshua from Egypt to the promised land. But God kept His promise; Joshua entered the promised land. He led the people to victory in many battles. He left a legacy of obedience to God. Joshua wanted the people to remember how God had sustained them along the journey and to always choose to obey God.

- *How can we show we love God? We can serve, worship, and obey God.*
- Jesus left His followers what legacy? (*He appeared to the disciples and left them with a legacy: to make disciples of all nations, baptizing them in the name of the Father and of the Son and of the Holy Spirit, teaching them to obey everything Jesus commanded. [Matthew 28:19-20]*)

If you choose to review with boys and girls how to become a Christian, explain that kids are welcome to speak with you or another teacher if they have questions.

- **God rules.** God created and is in charge of everything. (Gen. 1:1; Rev. 4:11; Col. 1:16-17)
- **We sinned.** Since Adam and Eve, everyone has chosen to disobey God. (Rom. 3:23; 6:23)
- **God provided.** God sent His Son Jesus to rescue us from the punishment we deserve. (John 3:16; Eph. 2:8-9)
- **Jesus gives.** Jesus lived a perfect life, died on the cross for our sins, and rose again so we can be welcomed into God's family. (Rom. 5:8; 2 Cor. 5:21; 1 Pet. 3:18)
- **We respond.** Believe that Jesus alone saves you. Repent. Tell God that your faith is in Jesus. (Rom. 10:9-10,13)

Key passage activity (5 minutes)

- Key Passage Poster (enhanced CD)
- index cards
- markers
- Print the key passage on index cards, one word per card. Create another set of cards using words not found in the key passage.

Reveal two index cards, one with the first word of the key passage and one with a wrong word. Instruct kids to choose the correct word. Reveal two more index cards, one with the second word and one with a wrong word. Repeat the pattern until kids have chosen all the correct words in order. Read the key passage together.

Say • Every day we have choices to make. Each choice is a choice to follow God or to follow something or someone else. The key passage reminds us of our big picture question, *How can we show we love God? We can serve, worship, and obey God.*

Activity choice (10 minutes)

Option 1: Ways to worship game

On separate pieces of paper, list four ways to worship God. Tape one to each wall to create a worship zone. Suggested ways to worship include prayer, singing, praising God while reading the Bible, thanking God for His blessings, serving someone, telling someone about Jesus.

- paper, 4 pieces
- marker
- tape or other method of attaching paper to wall

Say • *How can we show we love God? We can serve, worship, and obey God.* What does it mean to worship God?

Select one kid to be the caller. The caller will stand in the middle of the room with his eyes closed. The other kids will each move to a worship zone. Without opening his eyes, the caller will call out one of the ways of worship. Everyone standing in that worship zone remains in the game. Continue until one kid remains; he is the caller for the next round.

Say • We've talked about ways to worship God. What are some ways we can serve and obey God? How did Jesus worship, serve, and obey God?

• What did Jesus command His followers to do? (*Jesus appeared to the disciples and left them with a legacy: to make disciples of all nations, baptizing them in the name of the Father and of the Son and of the Holy Spirit, teaching them to obey everything Jesus commanded. [Matthew 28:19-20]*)

• small ball
• paper
• pencils

Tip: Play a second round with new answers.

Option 2: Initial toss-up

Explain that you will give each kid 60 seconds to think of a way to worship, serve, or obey God that starts with her initials. After 60 seconds, toss the ball to a kid and allow her to share her response. If she can't respond, she may toss the ball back to you and take a turn again later.

Play a second round, challenging each kid to provide her response within 10 seconds of receiving the ball. You may choose to allow kids to toss the ball to one another.

Say • *How can we show we love God? We can serve, worship, and obey God.*

• pencils
• journals
• Bibles
• Journal Page, 1 per kid (enhanced CD)
• "Books of the Bible Search" activity page, 1 per kid

Journal and prayer (5 minutes)

Lead kids to write or draw a prayer to God detailing how they will show they love Him by serving, worshiping, and obeying Him during the coming week. Encourage kids that sometimes we fail to serve, worship, or obey God, but God forgives us when we ask. He loves us and is gracious to us.

Say • How can you fulfill the legacy Jesus gave His followers?

Close in prayer asking God to help kids fulfill the legacy Jesus gave His followers.

As time allows, lead kids to complete the activity page, "Books of the Bible Search." Help kids identify which books are part of the History division of the Old Testament. (*Joshua—Esther*)

Unit 9: THE JUDGES

Big Picture Questions

Session 1: How does God accomplish His plan? God works in the lives of people to bring about His plan for redemption.

Session 2: What is the goal of God's plan? God's plan is to bring about His glory and our good.

Session 3: How should we respond to God's calling? We should obey God and trust Him to help us.

Session 4: What should I do when I sin? I should ask God for forgiveness.

Unit 9: THE JUDGES

Unit Description: Because His people continually fell into a pattern of sin, God raised up judges to help refocus the people's faith and trust in Him. God used the judges to help deliver His people from their enemies. While a judge was still alive, God saved the people from their enemies, but when the judge died, the nation would lapse back into sin and again need salvation through another judge.

Unit Key Passage: Judges 2:18

Unit Christ Connection: God used the judges to deliver His people from their enemies; Christ delivers people from the greatest enemy, Satan.

Session 1: The First Judges
    Judges 3:7-31

Session 2: Deborah and Barak
    Judges 4–5

Session 3: Gideon
    Judges 6–8

Session 4: Samson
    Judges 13–16

Teacher BIBLE STUDY

Following Joshua's death, the Israelites were without a leader. They fell into a cycle of sin that can be seen during each reign of the judges. The cycle is marked by an A-B-C-D-E pattern. Let's look at the first judge, Othniel, to see this pattern.

First, the people **A**bandoned God. They turned away and served other gods. (Judg. 3:7) Next, they experienced a period of **B**ondage. God was angry with the Israelites, and He gave them into the hand of the king of Aram. (v. 8) Third, the people **C**ried out to God. (v. 9) God sent a **D**eliverer to save them. (vv. 9-10) Finally, they had **E**ase in the land. (v. 11) Then Othniel died.

This pattern continued with Ehud. The people had again turned from God. Their abandonment made God angry. He sent them into bondage by strengthening the king of Moab to defeat Israel. The Israelites served the king of Moab for 18 years.

The Moabites were fat, especially the king. They enjoyed the fruit of the Israelites' labor while the Israelites went hungry. By thrusting a sword into the king's belly, Ehud disemboweled the king and left him dead on the floor of his room. The fat covered over the handle of the sword so that Ehud could not remove it.

After Ehud delivered Israel, the Israelites struck down the Moabites and there was peace in the land for eighty years. But Ehud would die, and they would need another judge to lead them. The Israelites needed someone better than a judge; they needed a king who would save them not only from the consequences of their sin, but the sin itself. That was all part of God's plan. God sent a true Deliverer; His Son Jesus died for our sin and delivered us forever from the oppression of sin and death.

Older Kids BIBLE STUDY OVERVIEW

Session Title: The First Judges
Bible Passage: Judges 3:7-31
Big Picture Question: How does God accomplish His plan? God works in the lives of people to bring about His plan for redemption.
Key Passage: Judges 2:18
Unit Christ Connection: God used the judges to deliver His people from their enemies; Christ delivers people from the greatest enemy, Satan.

Small Group Opening

Large Group Leader

Small Group Leader

The BIBLE STORY

The First Judges
Judges 3:7-31

Joshua had died. Without a strong leader, the Israelites began to disobey God and worship false gods. They forgot about the one true God. God was angry. He let an enemy king take over the Israelites, and they served the king for eight years.

Then the Israelites remembered how good they had it when they loved and obeyed God. They cried out to Him, "Save us!" God wanted the people to love and obey Him, so God raised up Othniel to rule over them as the first judge.

Othniel led the Israelites into battle against the king of Aram, and God helped the Israelites win. The land was peaceful for 40 years, then Othniel died.

Again, Israel forgot about God. God gave the king of Moab power to attack the Israelites and defeat them. The Israelites served the king of Moab for 18 years. The Israelites were sad. They remembered how good they had it when they loved and obeyed God. They cried out to Him, "Save us!" So God raised up Ehud (EE huhd) to save them.

The Israelites sent Ehud to the king of Moab, who was a very fat man. Ehud had a double-edged sword under his clothes. Ehud said, "I have a secret message for you." The king dismissed all his attendants so he was alone with Ehud.

When the king stood up, Ehud pulled out his sword. He pushed it into the king's belly. The sword was swallowed up by the king's fat. Ehud couldn't even pull it out! Ehud escaped down the porch, locking the doors of the room behind him. Ehud was gone when the king's servants came in. The door was locked and they thought he was using the bathroom. They waited, but the king never opened the door. The servants got worried, so they unlocked the door and found their king dead on the floor!

When Ehud escaped, he blew a ram's horn and he became the Israelites' leader. "God will help us defeat our enemies, the Moabites," Ehud told them. So the Israelites battled the Moabites and took control over them. There was peace in the land for 80 years.

When Ehud died, the Israelites forgot God again. They turned away from Him. When they remembered how good they had it when they loved and obeyed God, they cried out to Him, "Save us!" God sent a third judge, Shamgar (SHAM gahr), to save them.

Christ Connection: The judges saved the people from the consequences of their sin, but not the cause of it. God's plan was to one day send a true Deliverer—Jesus, His own Son—to be the King of His people. Jesus saves people from sin forever.

Small Group OPENING

Session Title: The First Judges
Bible Passage: Judges 3:7-31
Big Picture Question: How does God accomplish His plan? God works in the lives of people to bring about His plan for redemption.
Key Passage: Judges 2:18
Unit Christ Connection: God used the judges to deliver His people from their enemies; Christ delivers people from the greatest enemy, Satan.

Welcome time

Greet each kid as he or she arrives. Use this time to collect the offering, fill out attendance sheets, and help new kids connect to your group. Ask kids to share something they have planned for the coming week. What do they have to do to accomplish the planned activity?

- "One Letter Change" activity page, 1 per kid
- pencils

Activity page (5 minutes)

Lead boys and girls to complete the activity page, "One Letter Change."

Say • The three words you discovered are a part of our Bible story today. Have you heard of the word *judge* before? What do judges do today? In the Bible, judges not only made decisions to help people solve problems, they often served as military leaders. The judges helped save or deliver the Israelites from their enemies.

- paper, balls, buckets, hula hoops, masking tape (optional)

Session starter (10 minutes)

Option 1: Invent a game

Ask kids to create and play a game. Explain to the boys and girls that you will change the game if something is dangerous or someone could get hurt. Other than that, the game is up to them. Allow kids a few minutes to create. See if a leader emerges. If kids aren't working together, suggest they appoint a leader.

Say • Did your group have a leader? Who? How did he or she become the leader? Are leaders important? We will see today what happened when the Israelites had a leader and what happened when they didn't.

• assortment of unusual or random items of your choice
• gift bag or large paper bag

Option 2: Goofy grab game

Provide an assortment of unusual or random items. Place the items inside a gift bag or large paper bag.

Guide kids to take turns blindly selecting one item from the bag. Each player must share how that item could be used to bring glory to God. To bring glory to God is to bring Him praise, honor, or respect.

Say • God can use anything to bring glory to Himself. He can use a variety of things in His plan. He can also use a variety of people in His plan. Today we will hear about three people God used in unique ways to help the Israelites.

Transition to large group

Large Group LEADER

Session Title: The First Judges
Bible Passage: Judges 3:7-31
Big Picture Question: How does God accomplish His plan? God works in the lives of people to bring about His plan for redemption.
Key Passage: Judges 2:18
Unit Christ Connection: God used the judges to deliver His people from their enemies; Christ delivers people from the greatest enemy, Satan.

• room decorations

Suggested Theme Decorating Ideas: The theme this unit centers around judges on a reality show. Position a judges' table at the front of the room. Create a red carpet entrance by unrolling red fabric or long, red paper and securing it to the floor with appropriate tape. Hang long curtains or fabric behind your teaching area to represent theater curtains. If your ministry has spotlights or can lights, position them around the teaching area. You may also set up video cameras facing the judges table.

• countdown video

Countdown

Show the countdown video as your kids arrive, and set it to end as large group time begins.

Introduce the session (2 minutes)

[Large Group Leader enters walking down the red carpet, greeting kids along the way.]

Leader • Welcome! Welcome! I just love a red carpet entrance, don't you? It's so much fun! I need all my audience members to settle down. The show will begin very soon, and we have to finish our Bible story before the show begins. I just talked to one of the show's producers, and she gave me some great information to share with you. It's so exciting! The judges will arrive soon, and today's episode of "Do You Know the Bible?" will begin. Every week, the contestants compete to discover the answer to a very important question. The show calls it the big picture question. We're familiar with big picture questions, aren't we? Each week the contestants search for the answers to the big picture questions and the judges provide clues along the way.

Before we begin, I need to explain a little bit about the judges. Usually the show has two regular judges and a special guest judge. But today, all three of the judges are special guest judges. In fact, you may not have heard about them before, but all three are named after judges in the Bible. I'll tell you more about the judges in the Bible in a little while. First, let's review where we have traveled on our chronological journey through God's story.

• Timeline Map

Timeline map (1 minute)

Review the Israelites' journey to the promised land.

Leader • God's plan to send a Savior is so exciting to read and study! The Israelites finally conquered most of the promised land. They divided up the land, and each tribe went to live in its designated area. After Joshua died, the Israelites didn't have a leader anymore. A new generation was born, and the people didn't remember all the things God had done for them. What are some of the things God had done for the Israelites?

Call on a couple of kids to answer.

Leader • The new generation of Israelites did not remember all God had done. They sinned by choosing to follow false gods, and that is where our Bible story starts today.

Big picture question (1 minute)

Leader • The big picture question the contestants will try to answer today is, **_How does God accomplish His plan?_** Guess what? I am going to help you answer the big picture question before the contestants arrive. Open your Bible to Judges 3. The Book of Judges is in the Old Testament, after the Book of Joshua.

• "The First Judges" video
• Bibles
• Bible Story Picture Slide or Poster (enhanced CD)
• Big Picture Question Slide or Poster (enhanced CD)

Option: Explain the pattern using the A-B-C-D-E structure mentioned in the Teacher Bible Study. Be sure to explain all the terms in age-appropriate language.

Tell the Bible story (10 minutes)

Open your Bible to Judges 3 and tell the Bible story in your own words, or show the Bible story video "The First Judges."

Leader • Did anyone notice the cycle the Israelites practiced? First, the Israelites sinned by worshiping false gods and idols. Second, an enemy king conquered the Israelites as a consequence of their disobedience. Third, the Israelites cried out to God for help. Fourth, God sent a judge to lead the Israelites to defeat the enemy. Fifth, the Israelites had peace. Sin, Consequences, Help, Judge, Peace; Sin, Consequences, Help, Judge, Peace. This cycle happened several times in the history of the Israelites. We will see if it happened again before our study of the judges is finished. When the Israelites didn't have a leader, they began to sin.

We had three very interesting judges in our Bible story. Othniel was the nephew of Caleb. Does anyone remember who Caleb was? Right, Caleb was one of the twelve spies. He wanted to obey God and enter the promised land. Othniel was the first judge to lead the Israelites. The Israelites sinned, and an enemy king conquered them. They served the enemy king for eight years. The Israelites called to God for help, and God sent Othniel. Othniel was their deliverer. A _deliverer_ is one who sets others free.

God led Othniel to free the Israelites from the enemy king. The Israelites lived in peace for 40 years after Othniel delivered them.

Ehud was the second of the judges, and his story is very unique. Ehud was left-handed. He was also very clever in defeating the king of the Moabites. Ehud led the Israelites to defeat the Moabites. Israel had peace for 80 years after God led Ehud to deliver them from the Moabites.

The third judge of the Israelites was interesting because his story is exactly one verse long. Shamgar delivered the Israelites from the Philistines.

How does God accomplish His plan? God works in the lives of people to bring about His plan for redemption. God worked in the lives of each of the three judges we learned about today. Each time, God used them to help bring about His plan of redemption.

God wanted to save the Israelites, but God knew they would continue the cycle of sin. The Israelites needed a true Deliverer—one who could free them not only from the consequences of sin, but one who could free them from sin.

• Bible

The Gospel: God's Plan for Me (optional)

Leader •God's plan of redemption was to send His Son, Jesus, to pay the penalty for our sin. Jesus is our true Deliverer. He sets us free from sin when we trust Him as Savior and Lord.

Using Scripture and the guide provided, share with boys and girls how to become a Christian. Provide kids with an opportunity to respond by having counselors available to speak with kids one-on-one.

•**God rules.** God created and is in charge of everything. (Gen. 1:1; Rev. 4:11; Col. 1:16-17)

- **We sinned.** Since Adam and Eve, everyone has chosen to disobey God. (Rom. 3:23; 6:23)
- **God provided.** God sent His Son Jesus to rescue us from the punishment we deserve. (John 3:16; Eph. 2:8-9)
- **Jesus gives.** Jesus lived a perfect life, died on the cross for our sins, and rose again so we can be welcomed into God's family. (Rom. 5:8; 2 Cor. 5:21; 1 Pet. 3:18)
- **We respond.** Believe that Jesus alone saves you. Repent. Tell God that your faith is in Jesus. (Rom. 10:9-10,13)

Sing (4 minutes)

- "My Deliverer" song

Leader • Join me in singing our new theme song to our true Deliverer, Jesus Christ.

Lead kids to sing "My Deliverer."

Key passage (5 minutes)

- Key Passage Slide or Poster (enhanced CD)
- "As Long As The Judge Was Alive" song

Leader • Our key passage this month reminds us of the role of the judges. When the judges were alive, Israel followed God and lived in peace. Without a judge, Israel sinned by not following God. Read our key passage with me.

Lead kids to read the key passage together. Divide the room and lead half the kids to read the verse. Then lead the second half of the kids to read the verse. Sing "As Long As the Judge Was Alive."

Discussion starter video (5 minutes)

- "Unit 9 Session 1" discussion starter video

Leader • *How does God accomplish His plan? God works in the lives of people to bring about His plan for redemption.* In whose life can God work? Can God work in your life to bring about His plan of redemption? Watch this video and think about our big picture question.

Show the "Unit 9 Session 1" discussion starter video.

Leader • What do you think? In whose life can God work? Good answers! God can work in your life to bring about His plan of redemption. *How does God accomplish His plan? God works in the lives of people to bring about His plan of redemption.* What is a way God can work in someone's life to bring about His plan of redemption? We saw one way in our video. What is another way?

Allow kids to answer. Always affirm kids for responding.

Prayer (2 minutes)

Leader • Wow, we have had a busy day visiting the set of "Do You Know the Bible?" God used all three of the Bible judges to deliver the Israelites. Someone tell me one of the judges' names and how he delivered the Israelites.

Call on one kid to answer.

Leader • *How does God accomplish His plan? God works in the lives of people to bring about His plan of redemption.* I see it's time for us to leave the set of "Do You Know the Bible?" The guest judges need to come in and get ready for the show. The producers want to start filming in a few minutes. Come back next week, and we'll get a behind-the-scenes look at another reality show and meet another Bible judge.

After I pray, watch your small group leader for your turn to exit the theater and walk the red carpet on your way to small group.

Close in prayer.

Dismiss to small groups

The Judges

Small Group LEADER

Session Title: The First Judges
Bible Passage: Judges 3:7-31
Big Picture Question: How does God accomplish His plan? God works in the lives of people to bring about His plan for redemption.
Key Passage: Judges 2:18
Unit Christ Connection: God used the judges to deliver His people from their enemies; Christ delivers people from the greatest enemy, Satan.

- Bibles, 1 per kid
- Small Group Visual Pack
- markers or pens
- "Cycle of Judges Wheel" (enhanced CD)

Bible story review & Bible skills (10 minutes)

Review the three judges and ask the kids to identify the elements of the cycle of sin in the Book of Judges. (*sin, consequences, help, judge, peace*)

First, the Israelites sinned by worshiping false gods and idols. Second, another king conquered the Israelites as a consequence of their disobedience. Third, the Israelites cried out to God. Fourth, God sent a judge to lead the Israelites to defeat the enemy. Fifth, the Israelites had peace.

1. Othniel (Judges 3:7-11)
2. Ehud (Judges 3:12-30)
3. Shamgar (Judges 3:31)

Allow kids to label each section of the "Cycle of Judges Wheel" to reflect the cycle the Israelites practiced. The kids may draw on each section pictures of the Israelites during that portion of the cycle, or they may simply label each section with a brief description.

Say • *How does God accomplish His plan? God works in the lives of people to bring about His plan for redemption.*

• Who is the true Deliverer? (*God's plan was to one day send a true Deliverer—Jesus, His own Son—to be the King of His people. Jesus saves people from sin forever.*)

Review the timeline in the small group visual pack. Ask kids to point out one of their favorite Bible stories so far on the journey through God's story.

If you choose to review with boys and girls how to become a Christian, explain that kids are welcome to speak with you or another teacher if they have questions.

- **God rules.** God created and is in charge of everything. (Gen. 1:1; Rev. 4:11; Col. 1:16-17)
- **We sinned.** Since Adam and Eve, everyone has chosen to disobey God. (Rom. 3:23; 6:23)
- **God provided.** God sent His Son Jesus to rescue us from the punishment we deserve. (John 3:16; Eph. 2:8-9)
- **Jesus gives.** Jesus lived a perfect life, died on the cross for our sins, and rose again so we can be welcomed into God's family. (Rom. 5:8; 2 Cor. 5:21; 1 Pet. 3:18)
- **We respond.** Believe that Jesus alone saves you. Repent. Tell God that your faith is in Jesus. (Rom. 10:9-10,13)

Key passage activity (5 minutes)

• Key Passage Poster (enhanced CD)
• paper towel tube

Say • The Bible tells us Ehud was left-handed. Today we are going to play our key passage activity using only our left hands. I have a "doubled-edged sword" for us to pass. As the sword is passed to you and you take it with your left hand, say the next word of the passage.

Lead kids to say the key passage while passing the sword around the circle. To help kids, place the key passage poster on the floor in the middle of the circle. Instruct kids to find a new spot in the circle and repeat the activity.

The Judges

Activity choice (10 minutes)

Option 1: My life bucket toss

Say • God's plan of redemption was to send Jesus to rescue people from sin. God can work in your life to bring about His plan of redemption in the lives of others.

In our game today, we are going to think of ways God can use us to accomplish His plan. God wants us to share His plan of redemption with other people. Think of ways God can use you to share His plan of redemption in the places listed on the buckets.

Teams will take turns tossing a beanbag into one of the buckets. The other team will respond with one way God could use a person to accomplish His plan in that place. If the beanbag lands in the *other* bucket, kids can choose any location they might go (sports field, dance studio, friend's house, grandparents' house, and so forth).

Say • *How does God accomplish His plan? God works in the lives of people to bring about His plan for redemption.* God can work in your life to bring His plan of redemption to other people.

- beanbags, table tennis balls, or similar items
- paper
- marker
- tape
- buckets or pails, 3
- Label the buckets *home, school,* and *other.*

Option 2: Layered snack

Say • The Israelites had a cycle of disobeying God, facing the consequences, crying out to God for help, being delivered by a judge, and living in peace.

Today we are going to make a snack to remind us of the cycle the Israelites continued to follow throughout the Book of Judges.

Lead kids to create a layered snack and discuss what each layer represents.

1. cookie layer – sin of the Israelites
2. pudding layer – consequences of the sin
3. cereal layer – crying out to God for help

Tip: Post an allergy alert prior to class.

- crushed cookies
- pudding
- cereal
- whipped cream
- cherries or candy sprinkles
- clear cups
- spoons
- napkins
- allergy alert sign

4. cream layer – delivered by a judge

5. cherry topper or candy layer – living in peace

After all kids have assembled the layered snack, review the cycle again.

Say • Your layered snack is good. Was the cycle the Israelites practiced good? What was wrong with it? (*They sinned.*)

• *How does God accomplish His plan? God works in the lives of people to bring about His plan for redemption.* God used each of the three judges to deliver the Israelites. God can use you in His plan too.

Journal and prayer (5 minutes)

- pencils
- journals
- Bibles, 1 per kid
- Journal Page, 1 per kid (enhanced CD)
- "True or False" activity page, 1 per kid

Tip: Some kids may need encouragement to pray aloud.

Lead kids to write a prayer asking God to use them in His plan of redemption. Guide kids to record any prayer requests they may have. Kids may wish to write in code the names of people they are praying for.

Say • *How does God accomplish His plan? God works in the lives of people to bring about His plan for redemption.*

Ask each kid to voice a sentence prayer to God. It may be a prayer request, a thanksgiving, or a praise. Close in prayer after kids have prayed.

As time allows, lead kids to complete the activity page, "True or False," to review the Bible story. Help kids use their Bibles to find the correct answers.

Teacher BIBLE STUDY

The time of the judges continued after the death of Ehud. The Israelites fell into a continuous cycle of sin, bondage, deliverance, and peace. The people of Israel were oppressed by the king of Canaan. At this time, Deborah was the judge of Israel. Deborah sent for Barak and encouraged him to take up an army and fight the army of Canaan and its leader, Sisera.

Deborah reminded Barak that God would hand Sisera and his troops over to him. (Judg. 4:6-7) Barak agreed to go under one condition: that Deborah would go with him. Deborah went, but she informed Barak that he would get no glory for the battle; God was going to use a woman to defeat Sisera.

When Barak went down from Mount Tabor with 10,000 men, "The LORD threw Sisera and all his army into confusion with the sword before Barak" (Judg. 4:15). Everyone in the army died, but Sisera escaped on foot.

Sisera fled to the tent of Jael, who invited him inside and gave him a drink. While Sisera slept, Jael drove a tent peg through his temple and he died.

Judges 5 records a victory song Deborah and Barak sang on that day, praising God for defeating the Canaanites. The land had rest for 40 years.

The Israelites' sin had resulted in 20 years of defeat. God fought for the Israelites and used Deborah, Barak, and Jael to accomplish the Israelites' victory over Canaan. As you teach kids this week, use Psalm 115:3 and Romans 8:28 to help kids understand that God does whatever He pleases, and His purposes are for His glory and our good.

Use the Christ Connection to emphasize that God uses people and events to save us not only from our enemies, but to bring about our ultimate good: salvation through His Son, Jesus Christ.

Older Kids BIBLE STUDY OVERVIEW

Session Title: Deborah and Barak
Bible Passage: Judges 4–5
Big Picture Question: What is the goal of God's plan? God's plan is to bring about His glory and our good.
Key Passage: Judges 2:18
Unit Christ Connection: God used the judges to deliver His people from their enemies; Christ delivers people from the greatest enemy, Satan.

Small Group Opening

Large Group Leader

Small Group Leader

The BIBLE STORY

Deborah and Barak
Judges 4–5

Ehud and Shamgar had been judges over Israel. After they died, the Israelites forgot about God. So God allowed the king of Canaan to overtake them. The commander of the king's army was named Sisera (SIS uh ruh). Sisera was cruel to the Israelites for 20 years. God's people remembered how good they had it when they loved and obeyed God. They cried out to God, "Save us!"

Deborah was the judge over Israel at this time. One day, Deborah called for Barak and said, "God wants you to gather 10,000 men. Lead them to Mount Tabor. God will help you defeat Sisera there."

Barak said to Deborah, "I will go if you will come with me. If you won't come, I'm not going."

"I'll go," Deborah said. "But you will receive no honor for the battle." So Deborah, Barak, and 10,000 men went to Mount Tabor. Sisera heard that Barak was at Mount Tabor, and he took his 900 chariots and all his men to fight.

"Barak, go! God will help you defeat Sisera today," Deborah said. Barak and his 10,000 men moved down the mountain toward Sisera and his army.

The LORD confused Sisera and all of the army. Barak chased the chariots and the army, and everyone in the army was killed by the sword. None of them survived, but Sisera had escaped!

Sisera went to the tent of Jael (JAY uhl) because he and Jael's husband were friends. Jael said, "Come in. Don't be afraid." Jael gave Sisera something to drink and covered him with a rug. Sisera was so exhausted that he fell into a deep sleep.

Jael knew that Sisera was an evil man, an enemy of God. She took a tent peg and a hammer, and she drove the tent peg through Sisera's head, killing him while he slept.

Barak arrived, looking for Sisera. Jael greeted him and said, "I will show you the man you are looking for." Barak went into her tent and saw Sisera lying dead with a tent peg through his head.

That day, God allowed the Israelites to defeat the king of Canaan. The

Israelites had won the battle! Deborah and Barak sang a victory song. They praised God for helping them beat the Canaanites. The land was peaceful for 40 more years.

Christ Connection: God does what is for His glory and our good. (Psalm 115:3; Romans 8:28) God fought for the Israelites and used Deborah, Barak, and Jael to defeat Canaan. In a similar way, God uses people and events to not only save us from our enemies, but to bring about our ultimate good: salvation through His Son, Jesus Christ.

Small Group OPENING

Session Title: Deborah and Barak
Bible Passage: Judges 4–5
Big Picture Question: What is the goal of God's plan? God's plan is to bring about His glory and our good.
Key Passage: Judges 2:18
Unit Christ Connection: God used the judges to deliver His people from their enemies; Christ delivers people from the greatest enemy, Satan.

Welcome time

Greet each kid as he or she arrives. Use this time to collect the offering, fill out attendance sheets, and help new kids connect to your group. Invite kids to share about the past week. Did anything exciting happen? Did anything disappointing happen? Involve new kids in the conversation to help them connect to the other kids in the group.

Activity page (5 minutes)

• "Praise Puzzle" activity page, 1 per kid
• pencils

Guide kids to complete the "Praise Puzzle" to reveal two messages from today's Bible story.

Say • Both of these messages are part of a song the judge in our Bible story today sang to God. If you were singing a song of praise to God, what would you praise Him for?

Session starter (10 minutes)

Option 1: Paper chain bondage
Challenge kids to create the longest paper chain they can in five minutes. After kids complete the chain, ask them to stand close together and wrap the chain around them.
    Discuss the Israelites' bondage to other kings when they

• strips of paper
• tape
• markers or pens

sinned. Then allow kids to break the chain to be free.

Say • Once again, today's Bible story begins with the
Israelites in bondage. God sent another judge to help
the Israelites break free.

Lead each kid to write the unit key passage on one strip of
paper and tape it around his arm or leg as a reminder of the
consequences of sin.

Post an allergy alert
prior to class, even
if kids are not eating
any of the foods.

• various food items:
cereal, pastries,
canned vegetables,
candy, fruit cups,
chips, fresh fruit,
and so forth

Option 2: The good and the bad

Ask kids to sort the items according to what they think
is healthy and what they think is unhealthy. Discuss the
choices. Ask kids to sort the items again by what they think
is good to eat (they like it) and what they think is bad to eat
(they don't like to eat it). Discuss the difference.

Say • Is what we think is good to eat always healthy to eat?
Are some of the things that are good to eat (tasty)
unhealthy for us?
  Do we always know what is good for us in life?
Sometimes God knows something is good for us, but
we aren't sure it is good. God always does what is
good for His people. Listen to today's Bible story to
discover the good God wants for His people.

You may choose to allow kids to snack on one of the items
you brought.

Transition to large group

Large Group LEADER

Session Title: Deborah and Barak
Bible Passage: Judges 4–5
Big Picture Question: What is the goal of God's plan? God's plan is to bring about His glory and our good.
Key Passage: Judges 2:18
Unit Christ Connection: God used the judges to deliver His people from their enemies; Christ delivers people from the greatest enemy, Satan.

• countdown video

Countdown

Show the countdown video as your kids arrive, and set it to end as large group time begins.

Introduce the session (3 minutes)

[Large Group Leader enters walking down the red carpet. Pause and pose for photos along the way. Greet the kids.]

Leader • It's so fun to walk the red carpet! I know. How about I pick one of you to walk the red carpet? You can show us your poses and how you would greet your fans. Select one kid to walk the red carpet. Thank him for participating and send him back to his seat.

Leader • What fun! Welcome to the theater set of the reality show "The Great Bible Sprint." Today's contestants will compete by sprinting to various spots in the theater to answer challenging Bible questions and complete a series of tasks to be the first one to arrive at the answer to today's question. All of the contestants will be judged by the one, the only, special guest judge— Deborah. Deborah is a local judge who decides cases in a court of law and teaches the Bible each week at her local church, Palm Tree Fellowship Church. Today she will be helping the contestants on their sprint, and she will judge each task to be sure it is completed correctly.

Did you know the Bible tells the story of a judge in the Old Testament named Deborah? Our special guest judge Deborah reminds me of the Bible judge Deborah. Let me tell you more about the Bible judge Deborah.

• Timeline Map

Timeline map (1 minute)

Leader •Deborah was Israel's fourth judge. Who can tell me the names of the first three judges? Othniel, Ehud, and Shamgar were the first three judges of Israel. They each delivered the Israelites from an enemy.

Did they save the Israelites from the consequences of their sin, or did they save the Israelites from the cause of their sin? Right! The judges could only save the Israelites from the consequences of their sin.

Who can save us from the cause of our sin? Jesus! The judges were part of God's plan to send the Savior to redeem His people. The judges helped the Israelites see their need for a leader. Later God would send them a king, but for now He sent judges to deliver them.

Point to the pictures on the map of the later kings to help kids anticipate the upcoming chronology.

Big picture question (1 minute)

Leader •Deborah was a great judge and prophetess of Israel. She helped the Israelites know what God wanted them to do. She spoke for God. That is what a prophet or prophetess does; they speak to the people for God.

Who remembers last week's big picture question? *How does God accomplish His plan? God works in the lives of people to bring about His plan for redemption.* This week, the contestants on "The Great Bible Sprint" are competing to find the answer to our big picture question, ***What is the goal of God's plan?*** Last week we learned how God accomplishes His plan. This week we are trying to discover the goal of God's plan. I think I need to tell you about today's judge so you will know the answer to our big picture question.

Tell the Bible story (9 minutes)

- "Deborah and Barak" video
- Bibles
- Bible Story Picture Slide or Poster (enhanced CD)
- Big Picture Question Slide or Poster (enhanced CD)

Open your Bible to Judges 4 and tell the Bible story in your own words, or show the Bible story video "Deborah and Barak."

Leader • The Israelites once again lived the cycle we learned about last week. They stopped following God. The Israelites lived for 20 years under a cruel ruler as a consequence of their sin. They remembered the peace they had when they loved and followed God, and they cried out to God to rescue them again. God sent Deborah, a judge and prophetess, to deliver the people. Deborah called for Barak to lead God's people to fight the Canaanites. The Israelites defeated the Canaanites and lived in peace for 40 years.

Did you notice how the Israelites won the battle? God fought for them again. God confused the enemy's army and Israel won the battle. Do you remember our big picture question? On the count of three, I want everyone to tell me the big picture question. One, two, three.

Option: Ask an adult to share a testimony of a time God brought something bad to be something good for them. Make sure the testimony is kid friendly and age appropriate.

Pause and allow the kids to say the big picture question. If they are confused, gently remind them by giving them a couple of words to get started.

Leader • ***What is the goal of God's plan? God's plan is to bring about His glory and our good.***

Read Psalm 115:3 and Romans 8:28 to the kids or ask two small group leaders to come forward and read the verses.

Leader • By raising up a deliverer—a judge—to lead the Israelites to defeat Canaan, God received glory. Deborah and Barak sang praise to Him. The Israelites knew that God had saved them.

Remember, to bring God glory is to bring Him praise, honor, or respect. God received all of those things in today's Bible story. God also wants to bring about our good through His plan. It was for the Israelites' good that God delivered them from the Canaanites. God always does what is good for His people. Do we always recognize when God is doing something for our good? No, not always. Sometimes we don't see the big picture of God's plan right away. But God always works for His glory and our good.

• Bible

The Gospel: God's Plan for Me (optional)

Leader • *What is the goal of God's plan? God's plan is to bring about His glory and our good.* What is our ultimate good? Our ultimate good is salvation. God wants to bring about our ultimate good, so He sent Jesus to make the way for us to have a right relationship with God.
Share with boys and girls how to receive God's gift of salvation. Provide kids with an opportunity to respond by speaking with a counselor.

- **God rules.** God created and is in charge of everything. (Gen. 1:1; Rev. 4:11; Col. 1:16-17)
- **We sinned.** Since Adam and Eve, everyone has chosen to disobey God. (Rom. 3:23; 6:23)
- **God provided.** God sent His Son Jesus to rescue us from the punishment we deserve. (John 3:16; Eph. 2:8-9)
- **Jesus gives.** Jesus lived a perfect life, died on the cross for our sins, and rose again so we can be

welcomed into God's family. (Rom. 5:8; 2 Cor. 5:21; 1 Pet. 3:18)

- **We respond.** Believe that Jesus alone saves you. Repent. Tell God that your faith is in Jesus. (Rom. 10:9-10,13)

Sing (5 minutes)

• "My Deliverer" song

Leader • The Israelites won the battle and sang praises to God. They sang a song to Him as the God of Israel. They also said they hoped God's friends and followers would be strong or mighty like the rising sun.

Does anyone remember another time people sang praise to God after He helped them? It's one of the stories on our timeline map. Yes! Moses and the Israelites sang a song of praise to God after He parted the Red Sea. That song and the song in today's Bible story are ways the Israelites remembered what God had done. They sang about it.

Let's sing about our great God, our Deliverer.

Lead boys and girls to sing, "My Deliverer."

Discussion starter video (5 minutes)

• "Unit 9 Session 2" discussion starter video

Leader • Name a time when you might not understand how something is for your good. Good answers! Watch this video and try to decide if what is happening to the kid is for his good.

Show the "Unit 9 Session 2" discussion starter video.

Leader • What would you think if you were in that situation? Would it be hard? Do you agree with his parent? Why or why not?

Review Romans 8:28.

Leader • Is it hard to always believe this verse? Sometimes. We won't always understand how God is going to turn something bad into something good for us. But God knows what is best for us. God is good. Everything He does is good. *What is the goal of God's plan? God's plan is to bring about His glory and our good.*

• Key Passage Slide or Poster (enhanced CD)
• "As Long As the Judge Was Alive" song

Key passage (4 minutes)

Leader • Do I have a volunteer who would like to lead us in reading our key passage?

Select a volunteer to come forward and lead the group.

Leader • Do you think we can say the passage without looking at the words? What about the first two lines? Everyone study them for a few seconds. OK, let's try the first two lines. Good! Study some more at home this week and we'll have this key passage memorized in no time.

Guide kids to sing "As Long As the Judge Was Alive."

Prayer (2 minutes)

Leader • Deborah was a great judge and prophetess. God used her to bring about His glory and the Israelites' good. *What is the goal of God's plan? God's plan is to bring about His glory and our good.* Well, we are out of time today. It's time for us to depart the stage of "The Great Bible Sprint." The producers are getting ready to bring in the studio audience and the contestants. We have to go because we already know the answer to the big picture question. The producers don't want to risk one of the contestants tricking us into telling them the answer before the show begins.

After I pray, watch your small group leader for the signal for your group to exit using our red carpet. Come back next week to learn what show we will explore next.

Close in prayer.

Dismiss to small groups

The Judges

Small Group LEADER

Session Title: Deborah and Barak
Bible Passage: Judges 4–5
Big Picture Question: What is the goal of God's plan? God's plan is to bring about His glory and our good.
Key Passage: Judges 2:18
Unit Christ Connection: God used the judges to deliver His people from their enemies; Christ delivers people from the greatest enemy, Satan.

- Bibles, 1 per kid
- Small Group Visual Pack
- sand
- sand pails or containers
- toy sand shovel
- blanket, tarp, or large piece of paper
- Place the blanket on the floor under the sand to make cleanup easier.

Bible story review & Bible skills (10 minutes)

Kids should form pairs. One partner must close her eyes. She must transfer one shovel of sand from one pail to another pail. The second partner may not use his hands to assist. Allow each partner to take a turn.

Say • Is moving sand with your eyes closed a wise idea? Why or why not? What unwise choices did the Israelites make in today's Bible story?

Select a volunteer to read Judges 4:1. Review the Bible story by retelling the story or allowing kids to retell the story using the Bible as a guide.

- Deborah served the Israelites as a judge. (Judg. 4:4-5)
- Deborah summoned Barak. (Judg. 4:6)
- Deborah and Barak assembled the Israelite troops at Mount Tabor. (Judg. 4:9-10,14)
- Jael defeated Sisera. (Judg. 4:21-22)
- Deborah and Barak sang a song of praise. (Judg. 5:1-31)

Review the timeline in the small group visual pack.

Say • *What is the goal of God's plan? God's plan is to bring about His glory and our good.*

- What is our ultimate good? (*God uses people and*

events to save us not only from our enemies, but to bring about our ultimate good: salvation through His Son, Jesus Christ.)

If you choose to review with boys and girls how to become a Christian, explain that kids are welcome to speak with you or another teacher if they have questions.

- **God rules.** God created and is in charge of everything. (Gen. 1:1; Rev. 4:11; Col. 1:16-17)
- **We sinned.** Since Adam and Eve, everyone has chosen to disobey God. (Rom. 3:23; 6:23)
- **God provided.** God sent His Son Jesus to rescue us from the punishment we deserve. (John 3:16; Eph. 2:8-9)
- **Jesus gives.** Jesus lived a perfect life, died on the cross for our sins, and rose again so we can be welcomed into God's family. (Rom. 5:8; 2 Cor. 5:21; 1 Pet. 3:18)
- **We respond.** Believe that Jesus alone saves you. Repent. Tell God that your faith is in Jesus. (Rom. 10:9-10,13)

Key passage activity (5 minutes)

- Key Passage Poster (enhanced CD)
- large shallow container
- sand
- pencils

Allow kids to take turns using a pencil to write a phrase of the key passage in the sand. Each phrase should be two or three words. The other kids must then say the word before the phrase and the word after the phrase in the key passage.

Say • Why do you think the Israelites only followed God when the judge was alive? The judges helped the Israelites understand their need for a leader from God. God was preparing to send the Israelites a king.

Do you think you would follow God if you didn't have parents, teachers, and others leading you to learn about Him? Even when we don't have a human leader, God wants us to follow Him. We can always read the Bible and ask God for His guidance.

Activity choice (10 minutes)

Option 1: Step up

Form two teams. Ask teams to line up facing the leader. The leader will read a command from the Bible. The team member that steps forward first will be given the chance to share an excuse kids make for not following that rule.

• taped line (optional)
• Bibles (optional)

Step up commands:

1. Love the Lord with all your heart. (Matt. 22:37)
2. Love your neighbor as yourself. (Matt. 22:39)
3. Trust in the Lord. (Prov. 3:5)
4. Don't worry. (Matt. 6:34)
5. Go and make disciples of all nations. (Matt. 28:19)
6. Do not have other gods. (Ex. 20:3)
7. Do not lie. (Ex. 20:16)
8. Remember the Sabbath day. (Ex. 20:8)
9. Serve the Lord with gladness. (Ps. 100:2)
10. Give thanks to the Lord. (Ps. 107:1)

Say • Is any excuse for disobeying God good? (*No!*) Why do you think people choose to sin?

• *What is the goal of God's plan? God's plan is to bring about His glory and our good.*

• What is our ultimate good? (*God uses people and events to save us not only from our enemies, but to bring about our ultimate good: salvation through His Son, Jesus Christ.*)

Option 2: Game stations

Provide several game stations. Post a helper at each station or print the goal of each game and post it at the station.

• Supplies for the game stations you choose to offer.
• paper
• markers

Game suggestions:
- Toss a beanbag in the bucket 4 times.
- Hit the target with the ball in 3 tries.
- Keep a balloon off the ground for 2 minutes.
- Pop as many bubbles as you can in 30 seconds.
- Walk in straight line on a piece of tape without losing your balance.
- Ring a paper plate ring around a chair leg twice.
- Drop 7 out of 10 clothespins into a jar.

Direct kids to select one of the stations and play the game. Kids may change stations and play more than one game if time allows. After a few minutes, call kids back together.

Say • What was the goal of each station? Was it important to know the goal of the station in order to play the game properly?

• *What is the goal of God's plan? God's plan is to bring about His glory and our good.* Why is it important to know the goal of God's plan?

• What is our ultimate good? (*God uses people and events to save us not only from our enemies, but to bring about our ultimate good: salvation through His Son, Jesus Christ.*)

Journal and prayer (5 minutes)

- pencils
- journals
- Bibles
- Journal Page, 1 per kid (enhanced CD)
- "Deborah Crossword" activity page, 1 per kid

Instruct each kid to write a prayer asking God to help her trust that He is always good. Kids may look through their journals at past prayer requests and note any that God has answered.

Say • *What is the goal of God's plan? God's plan is to bring about His glory and our good.*

As time allows, lead kids to use the Bible to complete the activity page, "Deborah Crossword."

Teacher BIBLE STUDY

Judges 6 starts out in a familiar way: "The Israelites did what was evil in the sight of the LORD." The period of Judges was not a good time for the Israelites. Their cycle of sin, bondage, deliverance, and peace clearly showed they had not learned from their past mistakes.

The Israelites were oppressed by the Midianites, and they cried out to God for help. God chose a man to save them, and his name was Gideon. Gideon was an unlikely leader, and he knew this. Gideon said, "Please, Lord, how can I deliver Israel? Look, my family is the weakest in Manasseh, and I am the youngest in my father's house" (Judg. 6:15).

God doesn't need the biggest and the best to accomplish His plan. He doesn't rely on men to go forward. God had a solution to empower Gideon in his weakness: "But I will be with you," He said. (Judg. 6:16)

Gideon and an army of men assembled. God told Gideon he had too many men. God didn't want the men to think they had the power to defeat the Midianites themselves. When the army was reduced to just 300 men, they prepared for battle. (See Judg. 7:1-7.)

The men ran toward the Midianites' camp, blowing their trumpets and shouting. God turned the swords of the Midianites against each other. They ran away, but Gideon and his army chased after them and killed them.

God was with the Israelites when they went to battle. The Israelites did not win the battle themselves; God fought for them. As you teach kids this week, point out that God used Gideon in the victory. Gideon alone was not enough to save the Israelites. Only God could win the battle. In the same way, we are unable to save ourselves from sin. Jesus came to save us from our sin because He is enough. Only God, through Christ, can save us.

Older Kids BIBLE STUDY OVERVIEW

Session Title: Gideon
Bible Passage: Judges 6–8
Big Picture Question: How should we respond to God's calling? We
   should obey God and trust Him to help us.
Key Passage: Judges 2:18
Unit Christ Connection: God used the judges to deliver His people from
   their enemies; Christ delivers people from the greatest enemy, Satan.

Small Group Opening

Large Group Leader

Small Group Leader

The BIBLE STORY

Gideon
Judges 6–8

The Israelites did what is evil in the sight of the LORD, so God allowed them to be ruled by Midian for seven years. The Israelites tried to hide from the Midianites in mountains and caves. Anytime the Israelites planted crops, the Midianites attacked them. They took their food and left nothing for them to eat. The Midianites took away their sheep, oxen, and donkeys. Israel became poor. They remembered how good life was when they loved and obeyed God. They cried out to God, "Save us!"

God sent a prophet to them. A prophet is someone who speaks for God. The prophet said to them: "God wants me to remind you of all the things He has done for you. He brought you out of Egypt and saved you from slavery! He told you not to worship the gods of the land you were living in, but you disobeyed God!"

The Angel of the LORD came and sat under an oak tree. The Angel of the LORD appeared to Gideon and said, "The LORD is with you, mighty warrior!"

Gideon was afraid. His family was the weakest family in his tribe, and he was the youngest son in the family. But the LORD chose Gideon to deliver the Israelites from the power of Midian. He assured Gideon, "I will be with you."

That night, God told Gideon to tear down the altar to Baal, a false god. Gideon was then to build an altar and sacrifice a bull on it. So Gideon obeyed God, but Gideon did it at night because he was afraid of the men in the city.

The next day, the men in the city saw that the altar to Baal was torn down. "Who did this?" they asked. When they found out Gideon had torn down the altar, they wanted to kill him. Gideon's father stopped them. "Let Baal defend himself," he said.

Some time later, God's Spirit was with Gideon, and Gideon blew the ram's horn. All of the men in Gideon's tribe and in the northern tribes gathered behind him, ready to fight. Gideon still wanted a sign from God. "If You will deliver Israel by my hand, as You say, I will put fleece on the ground. If the fleece is wet with dew, but the ground is dry, I will believe You." That is exactly what happened—the fleece was so wet Gideon squeezed enough water out of it to fill a bowl! Again, Gideon asked for a sign. This time, the fleece was dry and the ground was wet.

God told Gideon that he had too many people with him. They let anyone who was afraid to go to battle go home. Many of the people left. There were 10,000 remaining. "That's still too many," God said. God made a test for the people. All of them were to go to the river to drink the water. Anyone who lapped the water with his tongue was sent home, but whoever knelt and used his hand to bring up the water could stay. Three hundred men remained.

The next day, they carried torches, blew their trumpets, and shattered the pitchers that were in their hands. The men ran down toward the Midianite camp. God turned the swords of the Midianites against each other. Everyone in the Midianite army ran away.

Gideon invited the people of Ephraim to join in the battle. They pursued the Midianites and killed some of them. Gideon and the 300 men continued across the Jordan. They were very tired. Gideon pursued the kings of Midian and killed them.

The Israelites said to Gideon, "Rule over us, for you delivered us from the Midianites."

"I will not rule over you," Gideon said. "God will rule over you." Gideon told the people to bring him the golden earrings they had taken from the spoil. He used the gold to make an ephod. Gideon sinned by making the ephod, and after Gideon died, the Israelites bowed down to it. They did not remember the LORD their God who had delivered them from the power of their enemies.

Christ Connection: The Israelites cried out to God because they knew they could not save themselves. Even Gideon was not enough to save them; God used Gideon to save His people but God fought the battle for them. The people needed someone who was mighty to save. Jesus Christ came to save us from sin because we cannot save ourselves. Only God, through Christ, can save us.

Small Group OPENING

Session Title: Gideon
Bible Passage: Judges 6–8
Big Picture Question: How should we respond to God's calling? We should obey God and trust Him to help us.
Key Passage: Judges 2:18
Unit Christ Connection: God used the judges to deliver His people from their enemies; Christ delivers people from the greatest enemy, Satan.

Welcome time

Greet each kid. Use this time to collect the offering, fill out attendance sheets, and help new kids connect to your group. Ask kids to share about their favorite movies.

Activity page (5 minutes)

- "Save the Situation" activity page, 1 per kid
- pencils

Lead kids to complete the activity page, "Save the Situation."

Say • What does it mean to *save* someone or something? To save someone is to rescue them from danger. In the Bible, the word *save* can also mean "to deliver from the power and consequences of sin." Only Jesus can save us from sin. When we trust in Jesus as Lord and Savior, Jesus saves us. We are rescued from eternal separation from God.

• What is the answer to the question at the bottom of your activity page?

Session starter (10 minutes)

Option 1: Trumpet, pitcher, torch game
Explain the rules to kids: pitcher covers the torch, torch burns the trumpet, trumpet shatters the pitcher. Create

motions for each object. Pitcher: hold an imaginary pitcher in your hand and "pour" water from it. Trumpet: pretend to hold a trumpet near your mouth and play it. Torch: hold the torch up in the air.

Form two teams. Each team will huddle and decide which motion they will make. Teams should line up facing each other. On the signal given by the teacher, each team must perform its motion.

Say • In today's Bible story, the Israelites faced another battle. They used a trumpet, a torch, and a pitcher in the battle. Listen closely to discover how today's judge told them to use each item.

Option 2: "Obey now" washer watch

• washers, 3/8-inch or larger
• permanent markers
• 8- to 10-inch lengths of jewelry cord, 2 pieces per kid

Say • Do we always obey immediately when told to do something? Why are we reluctant to go immediately and wash the dishes or clean our room or walk our dog? Which would honor God more—to obey eventually or to obey immediately? We are going to make a reminder to obey God and others immediately.

Lead kids to make an "obey now" watch.

1. Print the words *obey now* on the sides of the washer. (See the illustration.)
2. Fold one piece of cord in half and loop the loose ends through the folded end to secure cord to the washer. Repeat for the other side.
3. Help kids tie on the bracelet and trim the cord. Be careful not to trim the cord too short or it will be difficult to tie in the future.

Say • In today's Bible story, obedience to God is important.

Transition to large group

Large Group LEADER

Session Title: Gideon
Bible Passage: Judges 6–8
Big Picture Question: How should we respond to God's calling? We should obey God and trust Him to help us.
Key Passage: Judges 2:18
Unit Christ Connection: God used the judges to deliver His people from their enemies; Christ delivers people from the greatest enemy, Satan.

Countdown

• countdown video

Show the countdown video as your kids arrive, and set it to end as large group time begins.

Introduce the session (2 minutes)

[Large Group Leader enters walking the red carpet. Pause to wave at "fans."]

Leader • Who is ready for another behind-the-scenes look at a reality show? What was that? Are you ready or not? Oh good, you are ready! Today we are visiting the set of "Who Has Bible Skills?" Each week contestants demonstrate their Bible skills for the judges as they discover the answer to the big picture question, and our judges award the first one with the answer a special prize at the end of the show.

I have been talking to the producers of today's show. The most famous guest judge on this show is a guy named Gideon. But it took the producers forever to get Gideon to agree to be a guest judge. He wasn't sure he was the right person. He is going to be the youngest judge on the show. He wanted the producers to show him some kind of sign or proof that he is the right person for the job. Hmm. That sounds a lot like a certain judge in the Bible. Let's look at our timeline map to see if Gideon from the Bible is the judge in our Bible story today.

• Timeline Map

Timeline map (1 minute)

Leader • Israel's first three judges were Othniel, Ehud, and Shamgar. God sent each of them to deliver the Israelites and bring peace to the people.

Next, God sent Deborah to lead the people. She delivered them and showed that God's plan is to bring glory to Himself and good to His people. Today, our timeline says we are talking about Gideon. Oh good. The Gideon on this reality show reminded me a lot of the Gideon in the Bible, so I am glad we are going to talk about him today.

Big picture question (1 minute)

Leader • Today's show also has a twist: contestants are going to be eliminated until only a few remain to compete. Wait a minute! Wait a minute! Have I even told you about today's big picture question? ***How should we respond to God's calling?***

What do I mean when I say God's calling? *God's calling* is a phrase that describes what God has given someone to do. Sometimes it refers to a special job or assignment God gives someone. So our big picture question is asking us to think about what we do when God calls us to do something.

How should we respond to God's calling? Open your Bible to Judges 6 and we'll find the answer our contestants are going to be looking for today. Judges is the second book of History in the Old Testament. It follows the Book of Joshua.

- Bibles
- "Gideon" video
- Bible Story Picture
  Slide or Poster
  (enhanced CD)
- Big Picture Question
  Slide or Poster
  (enhanced CD)

Tell the Bible story (10 minutes)

Open your Bible to Judges 6 and tell the Bible story in your own words, or show the Bible story video "Gideon."

Leader • Gideon's story shows us again how the Israelites turned away from God. The Midianites ruled the Israelites for seven years. The Israelites really suffered and cried out to God to save them once again. Before God sent a judge, He sent a prophet. The prophet reminded the Israelites of their sin and the many things God had done for them before they turned away from Him.

After the prophet, the Angel of the Lord called Gideon to be Israel's next judge. But Gideon wasn't exactly sure he was the right man for the job. Gideon was afraid.

Have any of you ever been afraid to do something God wanted you to do? Maybe God wanted you to tell a friend about God. Or maybe you had to go against the crowd to obey God.

Gideon was afraid. When he obeyed God by tearing down the altar, he did it at night. When God called Gideon to lead an army to fight Midian, Gideon wanted a sign from God. God graciously gave Him a sign, and Gideon asked for another sign. God was again gracious and gave him the sign.

Eventually Gideon did lead the army to defeat the Midianites. God was responsible for the Israelites defeating the Midianites. After the Midianites were defeated, Gideon made a mistake. He made an ephod. An *ephod* is an apron-like piece of clothing worn by a priest. The Israelites began to worship the ephod. Although Gideon was supposed to lead the Israelites to worship God, in the end, he led them to worship an idol.

Our big picture question is, ***How should we respond to God's calling?*** The answer is, ***We should obey God and*** *trust Him to help us.* Did Gideon follow our big picture question and answer? He did eventually obey God, but he asked for signs and was afraid before he obeyed. Do you think Gideon trusted God at first? Interesting thoughts.

God used Gideon to judge the Midianites, but Gideon could not save the Israelites from their sin. Only Jesus can save people from sin. *How should we respond to God's calling? We should obey God and trust Him to help us.*

Discussion starter video (4 minutes)

• "Unit 9 Session 3" video

Leader • Could the Israelites save themselves from sin? No. Could Gideon save the Israelites from their sin? No. Could any of the judges save the Israelites from their sin? No. Watch this video and we'll discuss it.

Show the "Unit 9 Session 3" discussion starter video.

Leader • Was the kid ever going to have a bucket full of water? Why? The bucket had holes in it. Can people save themselves from sin? No. Who can save people from sin?

The Gospel: God's Plan for Me (optional)

Using the guide provided, review the gospel. Explain how kids can respond, and provide counselors to speak with kids who have questions or want to respond to Jesus.

• Key Passage Slide or Poster (enhanced CD)
• "As Long As the Judge Was Alive" song

Option: If a kid memorizes the key passage quickly, challenge him to also memorize Judges 21:25 or Hebrews 11:32-34.

Key passage (5 minutes)

Ask if a volunteer would like to say the key passage from memory. Allow a volunteer or two to attempt saying the key passage. Encourage or help each volunteer as needed.

Leader • Great job! We have only one more week in this unit. Work hard on the key passage at home, and we will see how many of you have it memorized next week.

Guide the group to read the key passage together. Lead boys and girls to sing "As Long As the Judge Was Alive."

Sing (5 minutes)

Lead kids to sing the unit theme song, "My Deliverer."

Leader •What is your favorite line in our theme song?

Call on three or four volunteers to answer briefly.

Leader •I am so thankful that Jesus is my Deliverer. He rescued me from my sin! Only Jesus could save me. Only Jesus can save you from sin.

Prayer (2 minutes)

Leader •Well, that is about all the time we have here behind the scenes at "Who Has Bible Skills?" The producers told me that the special guest judge Gideon will be arriving soon, and we need to be gone when he and his assistants arrive. Gideon will be helping the contestants discover the answer to the big picture question. Who remembers our big picture question and the answer?

Invite a few kids to provide the answer. Lead the entire group to say the big picture question and answer together.

Leader •*How should we respond to God's calling? We should obey God and trust Him to help us.* After I pray, watch your small group leader for your turn to exit by walking down the red carpet.

Close in prayer, asking God to help boys and girls respond to God with obedience and trust.

Dismiss to small groups

The Gospel: God's Plan for Me

Ask kids if they have ever heard the word *gospel*. Clarify that the word *gospel* means "good news." It is the message about Christ, the kingdom of God, and salvation. Use the following guide to share the gospel with kids.

God rules. Explain to kids that the Bible tells us God created everything, and He is in charge of everything. Invite a volunteer to read Genesis 1:1 from the Bible. Read Revelation 4:11 or Colossians 1:16-17 aloud and explain what these verses mean.

We sinned. Tell kids that since the time of Adam and Eve, everyone has chosen to disobey God. (Romans 3:23) The Bible calls this sin. Because God is holy, God cannot be around sin. Sin separates us from God and deserves God's punishment of death. (Romans 6:23)

God provided. Choose a child to read John 3:16 aloud. Say that God sent His Son, Jesus, the perfect solution to our sin problem, to rescue us from the punishment we deserve. It's something we, as sinners, could never earn on our own. Jesus alone saves us. Read and explain Ephesians 2:8-9.

Jesus gives. Share with kids that Jesus lived a perfect life, died on the cross for our sins, and rose again. Because Jesus gave up His life for us, we can be welcomed into God's family for eternity. This is the best gift ever! Read Romans 5:8; 2 Corinthians 5:21; or 1 Peter 3:18.

We respond. Tell kids that they can respond to Jesus. Read Romans 10:9-10,13. Review these aspects of our response: Believe in your heart that Jesus alone saves you through what He's already done on the cross. Repent, turning from self and sin to Jesus. Tell God and others that your faith is in Jesus.

Offer to talk with any child who is interested in responding to Jesus.

Small Group LEADER

Session Title: Gideon
Bible Passage: Judges 6–8
Big Picture Question: How should we respond to God's calling? We should obey God and trust Him to help us.
Key Passage: Judges 2:18
Unit Christ Connection: God used the judges to deliver His people from their enemies; Christ delivers people from the greatest enemy, Satan.

- Bibles, 1 per kid
- Small Group Visual Pack

Option: Instruct kids to raise their right or left arms instead.

Bible story review & Bible skills (10 minutes)

Say • *How should we respond to God's calling? We should obey God and trust Him to help us.*

Ask all kids to stand up. Explain that you will read a statement. If the statement describes Gideon, kids should stand on their right leg. If the statement describes Jesus, kids should stand on their left leg.

1. I am the youngest son in my family. (*Gideon*)
2. I am from the tribe of Judah. (*Jesus*)
3. I am from the weakest family in my tribe. (*Gideon*)
4. I healed many people. (*Jesus*)
5. I asked God for a sign. (*Gideon*)
6. I blew a ram's horn to gather the tribes together to fight the Midianites. (*Gideon*)
7. I tore down an altar to a false god. (*Gideon*)
8. I threw the money changers out of My Father's house. (*Jesus*)
9. God used me to save the Israelites from Midian. (*Gideon*)
10. God sent me to save His people from sin. (*Jesus*)

Help kids locate Judges 8:33-35 in the Bible and discuss the end of today's Bible story.

Review the timeline in the small group visual pack. Explain to boys and girls that God used many leaders (Moses, Joshua, Ehud, Deborah, Gideon) to save the Israelites, but none of them could save people from sin.

Say • Who can save us? (*Jesus Christ came to save us from sin because we cannot save ourselves. Only God, through Christ, can save us.*)

If you choose to review with boys and girls how to become a Christian, explain that kids are welcome to speak with you or another teacher if they have questions.

- **God rules.** God created and is in charge of everything. (Gen. 1:1; Rev. 4:11; Col. 1:16-17)
- **We sinned.** Since Adam and Eve, everyone has chosen to disobey God. (Rom. 3:23; 6:23)
- **God provided.** God sent His Son Jesus to rescue us from the punishment we deserve. (John 3:16; Eph. 2:8-9)
- **Jesus gives.** Jesus lived a perfect life, died on the cross for our sins, and rose again so we can be welcomed into God's family. (Rom. 5:8; 2 Cor. 5:21; 1 Pet. 3:18)
- **We respond.** Believe that Jesus alone saves you. Repent. Tell God that your faith is in Jesus. (Rom. 10:9-10,13)

Key passage activity (5 minutes)

- Key Passage Poster (enhanced CD)
- table tennis balls, 12
- egg carton, clean
- permanent marker
- timer (optional)

Write the key passage on the table tennis balls. Place the balls in a mixed-up order inside the egg carton. Challenge kids to arrange the key passage in the correct order. Time each player to increase the challenge.

Say • The Israelites lived in peace while they had a judge. When a judge died, the Israelites slipped back into a pattern of sin.

The Judges

• "Gideon Cube"
  (enhanced CD)
• tape
• scissors
• Assemble the cube
  prior to small group.

Activity choice (10 minutes)

Option 1: Gideon numbered cube

Form two teams. You may opt to allow kids to play as individuals. Guide teams to take turns answering review questions (with "Gideon Cube"). To determine the number of points the team will earn for a correct answer, teams will roll the cube.

    1 point: Altar

    2 points: Wool

    3 points: Trumpet

    4 points: Soldier

    5 points: Torch

    6 points: Jesus

Say • *How should we respond to God's calling? We should obey God and trust Him to help us.*

• The judges helped the Israelites understand that they needed a leader, someone to guide them and lead them to always follow God. God's plan was to send Jesus, the King of kings and Deliverer, to save His people from their sin.

• Could Gideon save the Israelites? No. God used Gideon to save the Israelites, but God fought the battle for them.

• Who can save us? (*Jesus Christ came to save us from sin because we cannot save ourselves. Only God, through Christ, can save us.*)

• air-dry clay
• toothpicks

Option 2: Clay pitchers

Guide kids to shape a pitcher using the air-dry clay. Allow kids to use toothpicks to etch designs into their clay pots. Encourage kids to include the phrase *Trust God* or *Obey God* in their design.

Say • How did Gideon and his men use the pitchers during the battle? (*They smashed them; Judg. 7:20*)

- Did Gideon trust and obey God? Did he hesitate? Why or why not?
- When God calls us, should we hesitate or delay in responding? What should we do if we are afraid like Gideon was?
- ***How should we respond to God's calling? We should obey God and trust Him to help us.***

- pencils
- journals
- Bibles
- Journal Page, 1 per kid (enhanced CD)
- "Gideon Acrostic" activity page, 1 per kid

Option: Consider providing magazines and allowing kids to cut and paste pictures into their journals instead of writing.

Journal and prayer (5 minutes)

Lead the kids to name some of the fears Gideon had. Guide boys and girls to write a prayer in their journals asking God to help them overcome their fears.

Say • ***How should we respond to God's calling? We should obey God and trust Him to help us.***

Close in prayer. Ask God to help boys and girls obey and trust Him without delay.

If time allows, lead kids to use the Bible to complete the activity page, "Gideon Acrostic."

Teacher BIBLE STUDY

Samson was the last of the major judges of Israel. He was born to parents who dedicated him to the Lord as a Nazirite after an Angel of the LORD announced that Samson would be born to save the Israelites from the power of the Philistines. Samson grew up, and God blessed him with great strength. But when Samson requested to marry a Philistine woman, his parents were confused. Samson was supposed to deliver the Israelites from the Philistines. Why would he want to marry one of them? But God had a plan in all of this. (See Judg. 14:4.)

As Samson prepared for the wedding, he gave a riddle to the men with him about an event that occurred on his way to Timnah. (See Judg. 14:9-14.) Days passed, and the men convinced Samson's wife to tell them the answer to the riddle. This action sparked a series of events that would lead to the death of Samson.

In his anger, Samson torched the fields of the Philistines. He used the jawbone of a donkey to kill 1,000 men. The Philistine leaders determined to kill Samson. When he fell in love with a woman named Delilah, they bribed her into telling them where Samson's strength came from.

A man came and shaved the braids from Samson's head. He lost his strength and became helpless. The Philistines gouged out his eyes and took him prisoner. They had him stand between the pillars of the temple. In a final plea to God, Samson asked for his strength back. God gave him strength, and Samson knocked over the pillars, collapsing the temple. In his death, Samson killed more Philistines than he had killed in his life. (Judg. 16:30)

Though Samson disobeyed God, God used him to accomplish His purpose of delivering the Israelites from the Philistines. Jesus would come as the last Deliverer, saving through His life and His death those who would trust in Him.

Older Kids BIBLE STUDY OVERVIEW

Session Title: Samson
Bible Passage: Judges 13–16
Big Picture Question: What should I do when I sin? I should ask God for forgiveness.
Key Passage: Judges 2:18
Unit Christ Connection: God used the judges to deliver His people from their enemies; Christ delivers people from the greatest enemy, Satan.

Small Group Opening

Large Group Leader

Small Group Leader

The BIBLE STORY

Samson

Judges 13–16

The Israelites disobeyed God, so God handed them over to their enemies, the Philistines, for 40 years. But not all of the Israelites disobeyed God. Some of them still worshiped Him. Two of those people were Manoah and his wife. One day the Angel of the LORD appeared to Manoah's wife and told her she would have a son. Her son would belong to God. God had special instructions for the baby's life: he should never cut his hair. God said, "Your son will be a Nazirite. He is going to save the Israelites from the Philistines."

Manoah's wife had a baby, and she named him Samson. As Samson grew, God blessed him. God gave Samson great strength.

When Samson grew up, he saw a Philistine woman he wanted to marry. He went to her town to talk to her. As he traveled with his father and mother, a young lion jumped out at him. Samson killed the lion with his bare hands. Samson did not tell his parents what he had done. After some time, Samson traveled again to marry the woman. Samson found the lion's carcass. A swarm of bees had made honey in the carcass. Samson scooped some honey into his hands and gave some to his parents.

The Philistines sent 30 men to help Samson prepare the wedding feast. He told the men a riddle:

> Out of the eater came something to eat,
> and out of the strong came something sweet.

Samson was talking about the lion and the honey, but none of the men could solve the riddle. They asked Samson's new wife to help them. Samson's wife cried until Samson told her the answer to the riddle. Then Samson's wife told the men the answer. Samson had been tricked! He was angry, and he left his wife.

Later on, Samson went back to get his wife. But her father had given her to another man. "I thought you hated her," he said. Samson was so mad that he went out and caught 300 foxes. He tied their tails together with a

Older Kids Bible Study Leader Guide
Unit 9 • Session 4
© 2012 LifeWay Christian Resources

torch and sent them out into the Philistines' fields. The foxes burned up the fields. The Philistines went to find Samson to punish him. The men of Judah had tied him up with ropes, but Samson was so strong that he broke through the ropes. He took the jawbone of a donkey and killed 1,000 men with it.

Samson escaped to the capital city of Gaza. The Philistines found him there and planned to kill him. Samson fell in love with a woman named Delilah. The Philistines talked to Delilah. "Get Samson to tell you why he is so strong," they said. "We will each give you 1,100 pieces of silver."

Delilah asked Samson why he was so strong. She tested him with seven fresh bowstrings and with new ropes. She tried weaving the braids on his head, but nothing took away Samson's strength.

Delilah begged Samson to tell her the truth, so Samson did. "If you cut my hair, I will not have my strength." Delilah sent for the Philistine leaders. They waited until Samson was sleeping, then a man cut his hair. Delilah woke him up. "Samson! Wake up! The Philistines are here to kill you!" But Samson's strength had left him. The Philistines seized him and made him blind. They took him away in shackles and made fun of him.

Samson's hair began to grow back. One day, the Philistines made Samson stand between two pillars in the temple of Dagon, the Philistines' god. Samson cried out to God, "Lord GOD, please remember me. Strengthen me once more." So God strengthened Samson. Samson pushed on the pillars and collapsed the temple. Samson and all of the Philistines in it died.

Christ Connection: God raised up Samson as the last judge to deliver the Israelites from the Philistines. Samson killed more Philistines in his death than he did in his life. Jesus came as the last Deliverer, saving through His life and His death those who would trust in Him.

Small Group OPENING

Session Title: Samson
Bible Passage: Judges 13–16
Big Picture Question: What should I do when I sin? I should ask God for forgiveness.
Key Passage: Judges 2:18
Unit Christ Connection: God used the judges to deliver His people from their enemies; Christ delivers people from the greatest enemy, Satan.

Welcome time

Greet each kid as he or she arrives. Use this time to collect the offering, fill out attendance sheets, and help new kids connect to your group. Invite each kid to share about his or her week.

- "Honeybee Match" activity page, 1 per kid
- pencils

Activity page (5 minutes)

Guide boys and girls to use the Bible to solve the activity page, "Honeybee Match."

Say • Our Bible story is about a judge who was a Nazirite. He was supposed to follow the rules you just read in the Bible. The Nazirite vow was a special commitment made to God. Before this judge was born, God told his parents that he would be a Nazirite. God had a special plan for this man.

- yarn, 2 rolls
- tape
- scissors
- toilet paper, 2 rolls

Session starter (10 minutes)

Option 1: Make a wig contest
Provide each team with a roll of yarn, a roll of toilet paper, scissors, and tape. Challenge teams to create a long hair wig for each person on their team in seven minutes.

Say • Today's Bible story is about a judge who never cut his hair because of his Nazirite vow to God. He was also a very strong man.

Option 2: Strong man relay

The game may be played in a single relay or in teams based on the number of kids in your small group. Place the barbell and key passage poster at one side of the room. Direct the kids to form a line on the opposite side of the room. Instruct each kid to cross the room and read the key passage aloud while lifting the barbell from the floor to above her head as she says the passage.

Say • Today's Bible story is about the last major judge in the Book of Judges. He is known for being a strong man. He is also known for some of the choices he made. Today we will examine the choices he made and how God used him to deliver the Israelites from the Philistines.

Transition to large group

Option: Play a game by asking each kid to wear his wig while walking from point A to point B. Kids may not hold their wigs in place. If a wig falls off, the player must put it on again and resume walking. Challenge the group to complete the game in a specific time limit.

• paper plates
• wrapping paper tube
• Key Passage Poster (enhanced CD)
• Prior to class, cut a hole in the paper plates and slide them on the wrapping paper tube to create a "barbell."

Option: Use a pool noodle and swim arm floaties instead of paper plates and a wrapping paper tube.

Large Group LEADER

Session Title: Samson
Bible Passage: Judges 13–16
Big Picture Question: What should I do when I sin? I should ask God for forgiveness.
Key Passage: Judges 2:18
Unit Christ Connection: God used the judges to deliver His people from their enemies; Christ delivers people from the greatest enemy, Satan.

• countdown video

Countdown

Show the countdown video as your kids arrive, and set it to end as large group time begins.

Introduce the session (2 minutes)

[Large Group Leader enters flexing muscles and posing with muscles flexed while walking down the red carpet.]

Leader • I have been at the gym pumping the old iron as they say. I've been building up my muscles because today we are behind the scenes at "Bible Obstacle Course." The contestants race through an obstacle course here on the stage and around the room to complete challenges of physical and mental strength. As the contestants race through the physical challenges of the obstacle course, they have to stop along the way to solve Bible puzzles in order to win the game.

The producers told me that they don't know what the puzzle should be today. He asked me what puzzle they should solve. What do you think? Do you have any ideas? What about the big picture question and answer? That's a great idea! I'll tell him to let the contestants solve a puzzle that shares our big picture question and answer, but first we need to discover our big picture question and answer. What group of people have we been learning about? The Israelites' judges.

• Timeline Map

Timeline map (1 minute)

Review the previous Bible stories from this unit.

Leader • What role did the judges have in God's story? God sent the judges to help the Israelites. The judges showed that the Israelites needed a leader. God later sent kings to lead the Israelites. And He sent Jesus to be the King of kings and our Savior. Jesus is the only leader to conquer sin and death.

Big picture question (1 minute)

As time allows, review the big picture questions and answers from this unit:

> • *How does God accomplish His plan? God works in the lives of people to bring about His plan for redemption.*
>
> • *What is the goal of God's plan? God's plan is to bring about His glory and our good.*
>
> • *How should we respond to God's calling? We should obey God and trust Him to help us.*

Leader • Today our big picture question is, ***What should I do when I sin?*** Our guest judge on the show today is the strong man winner of the year. He has amazing strength. That reminds me of our Bible judge for today. The judge in today's Bible story is Samson. How many of you have heard of Samson before? God gave Samson great strength. Samson's story teaches us a lot about sin and what we should do when we sin. Open your Bibles to Judges 13. Let's find the answer to our big picture question, ***What should I do when I sin?***

• Bibles
• "Samson" video
• Bible Story Picture
  Slide or Poster
  (enhanced CD)
• Big Picture Question
  Slide or Poster
  (enhanced CD)

Tell the Bible story (9 minutes)

Open your Bible to Judges 13 and tell the Bible story in your own words, or show the Bible story video "Samson."

Leader • God had a plan for Samson. Samson was to be a Nazirite from birth. His mom even followed special instructions to get ready for Samson's birth.

Did Samson follow God's instructions? No, not always. Although Samson sinned, God still used him to judge Israel. God used Samson to punish the Philistines for not worshiping God. God even used Samson's death to punish the Philistines.

The Philistines wrongly believed they could worship a false god and not face consequences. They did not believe God is the one true God. As a consequence, the Philistines died in the temple of their false god.

Our big picture question is, *What should I do when I sin?* The answer is, *I should ask God for forgiveness.*

Did Samson sin in our Bible story? Yes, he did. He broke his Nazirite vow more than once. Did Samson ask God for forgiveness when he sinned? We don't know. The Bible doesn't tell us. Samson's story helps us understand the importance of asking God for forgiveness.

Read our big picture question and answer with me. *What should I do when I sin? I should ask God for forgiveness.*

We need forgiveness because we all sin. God sent Jesus, the last Deliverer, to save people from sin. None of the earthly judges or deliverers were able to save people from sin. They could save people from the consequences of sin, but they could not rescue people from sin. Jesus never sinned, but He took the punishment for our sin. Only Jesus can rescue people from sin.

Key passage (5 minutes)

Invite a volunteer to say the key passage from memory. Ask for a small group leader to say the key passage from memory.

Leader • Great work, everyone! You have worked hard to memorize our key passage. We memorize God's Word to help us remember what the Bible teaches us about God and how God wants us to bring Him glory. What does our key passage tell us about the Israelites and how they brought glory to God? When the judge was alive, they did. But after a judge died, they didn't bring God glory because they worshiped false gods. Say the key passage with me.

Lead boys and girls to read the key passage with you. Guide kids to say the key passage from memory.

Sing the key passage song, "As Long As the Judge Was Alive."

Discussion starter video (5 minutes)

Leader • Do you ever say "I'm sorry" or ask for forgiveness from someone, but you aren't really sorry? Watch this video.

Show the "Unit 9 Session 4" discussion starter video.

Leader • Does this sound familiar? Have you said that before? Are we always sorry we sinned, or are we sorry we were caught sinning? Sometimes we're just sorry we were caught.

What about Samson? Do you think Samson was sorry all the times he sinned? Did he ask for forgiveness? We don't know, do we? Think about our big picture question. ***What should I do when I sin? I should ask God for forgiveness.***

The Gospel: God's Plan for Me (optional)

Using the guide provided, share with kids how to become a Christian. Provide counselors for kids to speak with one-on-one. Clearly communicate to kids how they can respond both in large group and after large group.

• "My Deliverer" song

Sing (5 minutes)

Leader • God sent Jesus to be the last Deliverer. Jesus' sacrifice provides salvation to all who trust Him as Lord and Savior. Stand with me and celebrate the deliverance from sin God has provided through His Son, Jesus.

Lead kids to sing the unit theme song, "My Deliverer."

Prayer (2 minutes)

Leader • Wow! We have had a great time visiting the set of "Bible Obstacle Course" today. I am sad to say this was our last visit to a reality show theater. The judges have taught us a lot about God's plan to send Jesus, the last Deliverer.

Our chronological journey through God's Word will continue next week. Next time we will travel to a new place to continue exploring God's story. We have many more stories to explore as we study God's plan to send Jesus to redeem people from sin.

After I close in prayer, watch your small group leader for the signal to take your final walk down the red carpet. Close in prayer.

Dismiss to small groups

The Gospel: God's Plan for Me

Ask kids if they have ever heard the word *gospel*. Clarify that the word *gospel* means "good news." It is the message about Christ, the kingdom of God, and salvation. Use the following guide to share the gospel with kids.

God rules. Explain to kids that the Bible tells us God created everything, and He is in charge of everything. Invite a volunteer to read Genesis 1:1 from the Bible. Read Revelation 4:11 or Colossians 1:16-17 aloud and explain what these verses mean.

We sinned. Tell kids that since the time of Adam and Eve, everyone has chosen to disobey God. (Romans 3:23) The Bible calls this sin. Because God is holy, God cannot be around sin. Sin separates us from God and deserves God's punishment of death. (Romans 6:23)

God provided. Choose a child to read John 3:16 aloud. Say that God sent His Son, Jesus, the perfect solution to our sin problem, to rescue us from the punishment we deserve. It's something we, as sinners, could never earn on our own. Jesus alone saves us. Read and explain Ephesians 2:8-9.

Jesus gives. Share with kids that Jesus lived a perfect life, died on the cross for our sins, and rose again. Because Jesus gave up His life for us, we can be welcomed into God's family for eternity. This is the best gift ever! Read Romans 5:8; 2 Corinthians 5:21; or 1 Peter 3:18.

We respond. Tell kids that they can respond to Jesus. Read Romans 10:9-10,13. Review these aspects of our response: Believe in your heart that Jesus alone saves you through what He's already done on the cross. Repent, turning from self and sin to Jesus. Tell God and others that your faith is in Jesus.

Offer to talk with any child who is interested in responding to Jesus.

The Judges

Small Group LEADER

Session Title: Samson
Bible Passage: Judges 13–16
Big Picture Question: What should I do when I sin? I should ask God for forgiveness.
Key Passage: Judges 2:18
Unit Christ Connection: God used the judges to deliver His people from their enemies; Christ delivers people from the greatest enemy, Satan.

Post an allergy alert prior to small group time. If an allergy exists, discuss the honey without tasting it or bringing it to class.

- Bibles, 1 per kid
- Small Group Visual Pack
- honey
- spoons
- wet paper towels
- bread (optional)

Bible story review & Bible skills (10 minutes)

Offer kids the opportunity to taste a bit of honey. Consider spreading honey on pieces of bread.

Say • How does the honey taste? Is it sweet? Does it taste good? What was wrong with Samson eating a little honey? He was an Israelite and a Nazirite, and the honey was inside a dead animal. Samson had to touch the dead animal's body to get the honey, and that broke his Nazirite vow and Israelite law. The honey was not the sin, but the sweet honey tempted Samson to sin and he did.

• Name one time God used Samson to punish the Philistines.

Guide kids to use their Bibles to locate an answer in Judges 13–16.

Say • Did Samson ask for forgiveness when he sinned? The Bible doesn't reveal that information to us. But the Bible is clear on what we should do when we sin.

• *What should I do when I sin? I should ask God for forgiveness.*

• Who is the last Deliverer? (*Jesus came as the last Deliverer, saving through His life and His death those who would trust in Him.*)

If you choose to review with kids how to become a Christian, explain that kids are welcome to speak with you or another teacher if they have questions. Allow kids to locate some of the Scriptures in their own Bibles.

- **God rules.** God created and is in charge of everything. (Gen. 1:1; Rev. 4:11; Col. 1:16-17)
- **We sinned.** Since Adam and Eve, everyone has chosen to disobey God. (Rom. 3:23; 6:23)
- **God provided.** God sent His Son Jesus to rescue us from the punishment we deserve. (John 3:16; Eph. 2:8-9)
- **Jesus gives.** Jesus lived a perfect life, died on the cross for our sins, and rose again so we can be welcomed into God's family. (Rom. 5:8; 2 Cor. 5:21; 1 Pet. 3:18)
- **We respond.** Believe that Jesus alone saves you. Repent. Tell God that your faith is in Jesus. (Rom. 10:9-10,13)

• Key Passage Poster (enhanced CD)

Key passage activity (5 minutes)

Challenge boys and girls to perform sit-ups, do jumping jacks, or jog in place as they say the key passage. For example: A kid would say one word when he sits up and one word when he sits back, or one word with jumping jack hands up and one word with jumping jack hands down.

• tape
• Bibles
• Create a tape grid on the floor with squares large enough for kids to stand in.

Say • God gave Samson great strength so he could deliver Israel. Samson judged Israel for 20 years. Samson is the last of the major judges in the Book of Judges.

Activity choice (10 minutes)

Option 1: Human tic-tac-toe

Form two teams. Allow kids to use their Bibles during

the game. If a team answers a review question correctly, a member of the team may stand inside one square of the tic-tac-toe grid. Play until a team wins or a tie is announced. Play again. You may also choose to ask review questions from other Bible stories in this unit.

1. Whom did the Israelites serve for 40 years? (*the Philistines, Judges 13:1*)
2. What was the name of Samson's father? (*Manoah; Judges 13:2-5,24*)
3. The Angel of the Lord told Samson's mother that Samson would be a _____. (*Nazirite, Judges 13:5*)
4. What did Samson kill with his bare hands? (*a lion, Judges 14:5-6*)
5. What did Samson later find in the lion's carcass? (*A swarm of bees had made honey, Judges 14:8*)
6. Who told the Philistines the answer to Samson's riddle? (*Samson's wife, Judges 14:17*)
7. Whom did Samson fall in love with? (*Delilah, Judges 16:4*)
8. How much silver did the Philistines promise to give Delilah if she betrayed Samson? (*1,100 pieces of silver each; Judges 16:5*)
9. Name one of the ways Delilah tried to make Samson lose his strength. (*tied him with seven fresh bowstrings; tied him with new ropes; wove the braids on his head into a loom; Judges 16:7-8,11-12,13-14*)
10. What did Samson say would take away his strength? (*cutting his hair, Judges 16:17*)
11. How did Samson die? (*He collapsed the Philistine temple, Judges 16:30*)

Say •*What should I do when I sin? I should ask God for forgiveness.*

Option 2: Braided bookmark

Allow kids to cut 12-inch pieces of embroidery floss or yarn. Kids may choose up to three different colors. If using embroidery floss, kids should cut six strands, two per color. The two strands should be grouped together and stay together through each step of braiding. For thicker string or yarn, only three strands are needed. Guide kids to braid the strings to make a bookmark.

Say • Samson lost his strength when his seven braids were shaved from his head. Cutting his hair was the only part of the Nazirite vow that Samson had not broken.

• Where did Samson's strength come from? The Lord gave Samson his strength!

Read Judges 16:20. Ask kids to respond to the verse.

Say • What does the verse reveal about Samson?

• Although Samson made mistakes, God used him to deliver the Israelites from the Philistines.

• *What should I do when I sin? I should ask God for forgiveness.*

Journal and prayer (5 minutes)

Encourage kids to write a prayer thanking God for His forgiveness. Guide kids to think about whether they need to ask God's forgiveness for any sin. Kids may also wish to ask God to help them resist sin.

Say • *What should I do when I sin? I should ask God for forgiveness.*

• Who is the last Deliverer? (*Jesus came as the last Deliverer, saving through His life and His death those who would trust in Him.*)

Close in prayer.

If time allows, lead kids to race a friend to complete the activity page, "Timeline Race."

• embroidery floss or yarn, multiple colors
• scissors
• tape

Tip: Tie one end of the strands together and tape it down on a table or other surface. This will allow the kids to pull the string tight as they braid.

• pencils
• journals
• Bibles
• Journal Page, 1 per kid (enhanced CD)
• "Timeline Race" activity page, 1 per kid

10 Tips for Teaching Boys

Do you teach boys in church? Here are some useful tips to make teaching a better experience for the boys and the teachers.

Provide appropriate choices

Boys need to be successful. To help them experience success, provide appropriate choices and allow them to choose the one that best fits their learning styles.

Make learning a game

Many boys excel in and enjoy playing games. Whenever possible, make a game out of a learning experience to challenge the boys.

Provide meaningful activities

Boys are passionate about certain topics. Find out what they are passionate about, and engage them in experiences that relate to those things.

Use technology

A sure way to keep a boy interested in learning is to introduce a topic through some form of technology. Provide Bible-learning experiences through computer games, music, videos, apps, and other appropriate forms of technology available in your church.

Allow opportunities for appropriate humor

Humor that is not degrading to another person will help boys feel more comfortable. Allow opportunities for appropriate humor each week. Learn to laugh, but set appropriate limits.

Provide male role models

Seeing men in areas of leadership, particularly in Bible study classes, will help boys grow in understanding by leaps and bounds. Invite men into your classroom, if only for one week, to engage the boys you teach and to give them the opportunity to see men involved in furthering God's kingdom work.

Build good personal relationships

Take some time to get to know the boys you teach. You will be surprised how they begin to respond when you get down on their level and ask them genuine questions about their lives. It may take some time, but they will begin to share.

> When you see a boy doing something well, make sure he is praised and encouraged.

Create opportunities to move

Many boys learn best when they are given opportunities to move as they learn.

Provide encouragement for the things they do well

When you see a boy doing something well, make sure he is praised and encouraged for that thing. Research proves that behavior that is noticed is the behavior that is continued.

Provide hands-on learning experiences

We know that boys like to move. Boys are experiential learners and will remember what they have done when they participate in the experience. Provide opportunities for them to touch or hold something as they learn.

Excerpted from *Bible Teaching for Kids 3rd and 4th graders Leader Guide*, Volume 3 Number 4.

Crossing the Culture

Webster's New Thesaurus of the English Language defines *culture* in two ways. First, as "a high level of taste and enlightenment as a result of extensive intellectual training," listing *courtesy*, *manners*, and *politeness* as related words. Second, as "the way people live at a particular time and place," such as a civilization with certain customs or lifestyles.

As a teacher of preschoolers whose families are preparing to live cross-culturally as missionaries, I strive to lay a foundation that blends together these two definitions. To help a child learn the importance of treating people of other nationalities who have different customs and lifestyles in a kind, courteous, and respectful way is to help them become children after God's own heart. (Acts 13:22)

Do not mistakenly think this is important only for children who will be living internationally.

You only have to walk around a neighborhood or through the local store to see that God has brought the nations together where you live. It is never too early to expose a child to the amazing plan God has for all mankind and how each person plays a part in that plan.

As teachers, ministers, and parents, we have the responsibility and privilege to teach young children about the diversity in God's world, and how we were created to join Him in sharing His love with ALL people. However, it is difficult to truly teach something if we do not believe it ourselves. Therefore, let's see what God's Word says and prayerfully ask Him to "know my heart ... see if there is any offensive way in me" (Psalm 139:23-24).

Biblical Foundations

All throughout the Bible, God is clear about His love for people—all people. Read Psalm 139:1-16 as a reminder of the astounding love God has for us before we are even born, the amazing way we are created within our mother's womb, and the passionate way God never lets us out of His sight.

Check out the familiar John 3:16, God loves the world so much that He gave the ultimate gift, His only Son. That promise is for the whole world, not just those who look and act like us.

Glance into the life of Jesus and see a man filled with compassion for the rich, young ruler (Luke 18:18-23), all the while rubbing elbows with those despised for their differences by the religious leaders of the day. There are Matthew (Matthew 9:9-13) and Zacchaeus (Luke 19:1-10), both tax collectors. There are Peter and Andrew who were lowly fishermen. (Matthew 4:18-20) There are the lepers, considered unclean by everyone but Jesus. (Luke 17:11-19) And yes, there are even noisy, rambunctious children! (Mark 10:13-16) Jesus loved them all, regardless of their stature, skin color, level of education or station in life. He even loved the people who ridiculed Him as He took His last breaths. (Luke 23:34)

> ...introduce kids to different cultures while teaching them to love all people with the passion of Jesus.

Finally, think about God's command to us to love Him and to love our neighbors as found in Matthew 22:36-39 and His commission for us in Acts 1:8 to be witnesses of His amazing love throughout the world. God gave us the perfect example of love and servant leadership in His Son, Jesus.

We will experience great blessing as servant leaders if we pass that heritage on to the kids with whom we live and minister. Let's explore some practical ways to introduce kids to different cultures while teaching them to love all people with the passion of Jesus.

Read About Other Cultures

Reading books to young children from the time they are born is one of the most beneficial things that can be done for them. This is true as well when teaching about other cultures.

Even a very young child who may not have the necessary motor skills or brain development to participate in complicated learning activities can still learn many things about the world and others through books. Additionally, by encouraging a love for books and reading, the possibilities are limitless of what children can discover about the people of the world.

For books exploring this topic, take time to visit your church media center or local Christian bookstores. Resources are also available at the public library or secular bookstores, but make sure the books are not contrary to the values set forth in the Bible.

Last, but certainly not least, remember the stories of Jesus! Reading from a colorful illustrated Bible story book is enjoyable for a child. However, never underestimate the value of reading directly from the Bible itself. This tells a child that the Bible is a special book.

Plan Activities to Teach About Other Cultures

As kids get older, they develop skills that enable them to take a more active role in learning about other cultures of the world. Let's

face it, kids and activities just go together!

Allowing kids to do art projects that are fun and informational is a great way to teach them about another culture. As always, remember that with any art, it is the process that matters and not the product. Here are a few ideas:

➤ In Germany, children are given a large cone shaped container filled with treats to celebrate the beginning of a school year. What a fun way to let a child begin a new year by making a cone out of construction paper, decorating it in a special way and filling it with treats.

➤ Children love animals! After reading books about animals native to other countries, allow a child to use clay to shape an animal of their choice.

➤ In Africa, many of the people groups enjoy wearing jewelry. Give a child a piece of yarn, several beads, buttons or two-inch pieces of a drinking straw to make a necklace or bracelet.

Learn a New Language

Common to most cross-cultural living is learning a new language. Factor in that studies in brain